International Students and Academic Libraries: Initiatives for Success

Edited by
Pamela A. Jackson
Patrick Sullivan

Association of College and Research Libraries
A division of the American Library Association
Chicago, Illinois 2011

The paper used in this publication meets the minimum requirements of American National Standard for Information Sciences–
Permanence of Paper for Printed Library Materials, ANSI Z39.48-
1992. ∞

ISBN 978-0-8389-8593-9

Printed in the United States of America.

15 14 13 12 11   5 4 3 2 1

Table of Contents

v   Introduction
Pamela Jackson and Patrick Sullivan

1   Chapter 1. Knowing Their Background First: Understanding Prior Library Experiences of International Students
John Hickok

19   Chapter 2. Engaging International Students Before Welcome Week
Jannelle Ruswick

45   Chapter 3. Creating Research Ambassadors: Expanding the Role of International Students
Elys Kettling Law and Nicola Kille

69   Chapter 4. Engaging International Students in Academic Library Initiatives for their Peers
Dawn Amsberry and Loanne Snavely

83   Chapter 5. International Education Week: Celebrating the Benefits of International Education and Exchange
Alena Aissing

93   Chapter 6. Beyond the One-Shot Instruction Session: Semester-long Partnerships for International Student Success
Amy R. Hofer and Margot Hanson

115   Chapter 7. A Multifaceted Model of Outreach and Instruction for International Students
Merinda Kaye Hensley and Emily Love

135   Chapter 8. Connecting to International Students in Their Languages: Innovative Bilingual Library Instruction in Academic Libraries
Eileen K. Bosch and Valeria E. Molteni

151   Chapter 9. Addressing Academic Integrity: Perspectives From Virginia Commonwealth University in Qatar
Nancy Fawley

165   Chapter 10. Addressing Deeper Issues of Information Literacy in Graduate International Students: A Korean Student Case Study
William Badke

185   Chapter 11. Connecting@ZSR: Meeting the Research Needs of International Graduate Students
Sarah H. Jeong and H. David "Giz" Womack

201   Chapter 12. An Integrated Approach to Supporting International Students at the University of Technology, Sydney in Australia
Dr. Alex Byrne

213   Chapter 13. The University of Southern California's Campus-wide Strategies to Reach International Students
Shahla Bahavar, Najwa Hanel, Karen Howell, and Norah Xiao

233   About the Editors

Introduction

Pamela A. Jackson and Patrick Sullivan

This book presents case studies of academic library initiatives that support the library, research, and information literacy needs of international students. The target audiences for this book are librarians and student service professionals who have a desire to more effectively reach out to international students on their campuses. The case studies offer varied perspectives and replicable ideas about how to encourage international students to use the library and increase international student success.

International Students in Context

According to data in the Open Doors 2010 report, the number of international students studying on campuses in the United States is at an all-time high. International student enrollment in U.S. institutions has steadily increased over the past five decades. The number of international students studying in the United States rose 2.9% from 2008-09 to 2009-10, to a total of 690,923 students. Approximately 3.5% of all U.S. college students are international students (national average), while on some campuses represented in our case studies, such as the Illinois Institute of Technology, as much as 40% of the total student body is international. The University of Southern California is the top host institution in the United States, with 7,987 international students, and California is top host state with a total of 94,279 students from other countries.

The top five countries that send international students to study in the United States are China, India, South Korea, Canada, and Taiwan. Eighteen and a half percent of the total U.S. international student enrollment is from China (up dramatically by 29.9% from the previous year) and 15.2% are from India (up 1.6% from the previous year).

According to the Open Doors 2010 report: "Together, the top three sending countries—China, India, and South Korea—comprise nearly half (44%) of the total international enrollments in U.S. higher education. Canada, Taiwan and Japan each represent close to 4% of the total international student population, with these top six places of origin comprising 56%." While Saudi Arabia only makes up 2.3% of the total international student population in the U.S., it is worth noting that enrollment of Saudi students increased dramatically by 24.9% from the previous year.

Top Countries of Origin for International Students Studying in the U.S. (2009/2010)

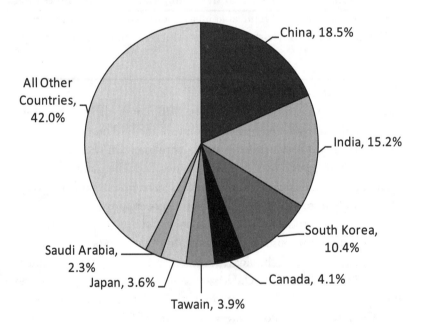

International students come to study in the United States in all fields; however, the top five fields are: Business and Management (21.1%); Engineering (18.4%); Physical and Life Sciences (8.9%); Math and Computer Science (8.8%); and Social Sciences (8.7%). These five areas account for 65.9% of all international students' fields of study.

Top Areas of Study for International Students in the U.S. (2009/2010)

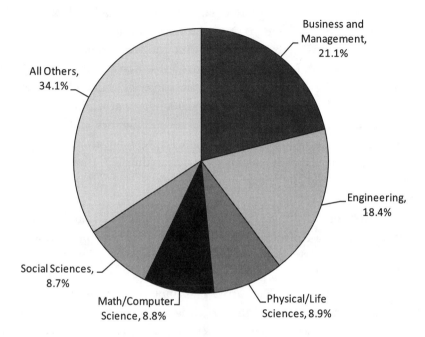

International students bring with them special skills and insights, but they also present unique challenges for our educational systems. Libraries play a critical role in connecting these foreign students, not only to our universities and colleges, but also to the information literacy skills they will need to succeed. Many students have not previously had librarians available to assist with their research. They are often unaware of library resources and services, and unfamiliar with academic jargon and Western library systems. It is therefore critical that we clarify the role that librarians can play in their educational careers.

The Case Studies

The case studies describe over a dozen exciting library projects that support the success of international students studying at academic institutions, and provide numerous examples of new and innovative strategies for librarians.

In Chapter 1, "Knowing Their Background First: Understanding Prior Library Experiences of International Students," John Hickok describes his sabbatical and grant project to investigate libraries in East and Southeast Asia. By interacting with and interviewing librarians and students from Indonesia, Vietnam, China, Korea, and The Philippines, Hickok gained a unique understanding of cultural differences. This provided a bridge for international students at California State University, Fullerton between U.S. academic libraries and those in their home countries. While international travel is not always possible, Hickok observed that developing an understanding of the international students' cultural and educational backgrounds strengthens strategies for instruction and outreach.

In Chapter 2, "Engaging International Students Before Welcome Week," Jannelle Ruswick describes a program at the Illinois Institute of Technology to reach out to international students before Welcome Week, the week before classes officially start. Ruswick found that many international students arrive on campus as early as 30 days before the start of classes and that exposing them to library services and resources early may help relieve anxiety, make them feel more welcome, and position the library as an inviting cultural hub.

In Chapter 3, "Creating Research Ambassadors: Expanding the Role of International Students," Elys Kettling Law and Nicola Kille describe an initiative called the Research Ambassadors program, an extension of the Wooster College Ambassadors Program. Undergraduate international student Research Ambassadors work closely with librarians to reflect on and share their experiences using libraries and conducting research in their home countries, and comparing it with their experiences as students at Wooster College.

In Chapter 4, "Engaging International Students in Academic Library Initiatives for their Peers," Dawn Amsberry and Loanne Snavely describe an international student internship program at Penn State University, which focuses on library services to students from China. Student interns selected materials for a new collection of popular Chinese literature, created an audio tour in Chinese, and reached out to their student peers using various social networking tools. The authors concluded that working with the interns gave the library new insight into their international student population and gave the students real-world experience and the opportunity to share their culture.

In Chapter 5, "International Education Week: Celebrating the Benefits of International Education and Exchange," Alena Aissing describes a variety of cultural activities hosted by the University of Florida libraries during International Education Week (IEW). IEW, a joint initiative of the United States Departments of State and Education, is held every November worldwide to celebrate the benefits of international education. Aissing found that participating in campus-wide IEW activities strengthened the library's partnerships with international studies offices and positioned the library as a hub for cross-cultural education.

In Chapter 6, "Beyond the One-Shot Instruction Session: Semester-long Partnerships for International Student Success," Amy R. Hofer and Margot Hanson describe a collaborative effort between librarians and instructors to integrate information literacy into the curriculum of the Preparation in Language and University Studies (PLUS) program at Golden Gate University. The authors worked as curriculum-building partners to embed library instruction into the program. They found that the instruction helped international students build information literacy skills in topic development, selecting appropriate resources, and evaluating information.

In Chapter 7, "A Multifaceted Model of Outreach and Instruction for International Students," Merinda Kaye Hensley and Emily Love describe a six-part instruction and outreach initiative for international students at University of Illinois at Urbana-Champaign. Through staff development, campus partnerships, and a variety of outreach, instruction, and cultural activities, the authors were able to better prepare international students for life at a U.S. academic institution and also open a conversation about cultural diversity with domestic students, staff, and faculty.

In Chapter 8, "Connecting to International Students in Their Languages: Innovative Bilingual Library Instruction in Academic Libraries," Eileen K. Bosch and Valeria E. Molteni describe a case study at

California State Universities Long Beach and Dominguez Hills in which library instruction was conducted in Spanish. They discovered that providing a welcoming and culturally appropriate learning environment raised students' comfort levels with conducting research in the library.

In Chapter 9, "Addressing Academic Integrity: Perspectives from Virginia Commonwealth University in Qatar," Nancy Fawley describes a specialized course at the Virginia Commonwealth University in Qatar to help international students understand academic integrity at an American university. She found that strong cultural differences and disparate educational philosophies shaped international student viewpoints on plagiarism, citing sources, and other ethical issues of academic integrity.

In Chapter 10, "Addressing Deeper Issues of Information Literacy in Graduate International Students: A Korean Student Case Study," William Badke describes his efforts to raise research skills among Korean graduate students studying at Trinity Western University in Vancouver, British Columbia, Canada. His intensive instructional efforts include teaching credit-bearing courses and workshops, translating instructional content into other languages, and exploring different cultural approaches to research, writing, and information literacy.

In Chapter 11, "Connecting@ZSR: Meeting the Research Needs of International Graduate Students," Sarah H. Jeong and H. David "Giz" Womack describe two programs for international graduate students at Wake Forest University, "Connecting@ZSR" and "Research@ZSR." Offered in conjunction with orientation events for all new graduate students, international students are given special tours, instruction on using the research databases, exposure to U.S. library terminology, and instruction on intellectual property issues.

In Chapter 12, "An Integrated Approach to Supporting International Students at the University of Technology, Sydney in Australia," Dr. Alex Byrne describes initiatives to support international students at the University of Technology, Sydney (UTS), where close to 25% of the student body is from countries other than Australia. Byrne details initiatives for international students, such as reading clubs to raise English language skills, services in other languages, and multilingual collections. He found that the programs at UTS library made international students feel more secure and welcome while studying in a foreign land.

In Chapter 13, "The University of Southern California's Campus-wide Strategies to Reach International Students," Shahla Bahavar, Najwa Hanel, Karen Howell, and Norah Xiao describe university-wide initiatives at the University of Southern California (USC) to reach international students. The authors detail international student orientation activities, collaborations between the library and various academic and student support departments, and library tutorials and webpages that support international student success.

The international case studies presented here, examine recommendations covering a wide range of innovative ideas. Many of these suggestions are direct responses to the rapid enrollment growth of international students on our campuses. The impact of these students is felt not only in the services we offer them, but also in the role the students play as library ambassadors in reaching out to other international students. Through the use of translators, whether professionals or international students, we can provide targeted services in their native languages, at the very beginning of their academic careers, when a little extra help may be needed to understand what our libraries offer. Another creative outreach strategy is the use of our international faculty on campus, both to connect with student populations from similar language and cultural groups, and to provide critical cultural education to library employees about the student groups we serve. Through connections with international student clubs, and incorporation of international students in collection development decisions, we can reinforce these bonds and, at the same time, strengthen our international collections and services. Finally, our international energies should not be confined to the library or limited to campus efforts. Connecting the library to the local communities that support our international students, and partnering with the very institutions from which these international students come, are but a couple of the strategies that we could explore. We look forward to librarians incorporating some of the concepts presented in these case studies into their own campus efforts. Hopefully, we will see some of these ideas and others reflected in future publications, providing an ever-expanding insight into future library services for international students.

Acknowledgments

We would like to thank Kathryn Deiss, Content Strategist at ACRL for her dedicated support and mentoring. Her enthusiasm for both the topic and for assisting us in seeing the project through to fruition was inspiring. We are very grateful for the opportunity to work with her.

Many thanks to the authors of these chapters. Their passion for supporting the academic success of international students studying at their institutions shone brightly, and their willingness to share their creative, exciting, and inspiring ideas is deeply appreciated.

References

Institute of International Education. 2010. "Open Doors." Open Doors. http://www.iie.org/en/Research-and-Publications/Open-Doors.

Further Readings

Association of College & Research Libraries (ACRL). "Academic Library Services to International Students Interest Group." Accessed April 12, 2011. http://www.ala.org/ala/mgrps/divs/acrl/resources/leadership/interestgrps/acr-igalsis.cfm

NAFSA: Association of International Educators. "NAFSA." Accessed April 12, 2011. http://www.nafsa.org/about/default.aspx

U.S. Department of State, Bureau of Educational and Cultural Affairs and the U.S. Department of Education. 2011. "International Education Week." Accessed April 12, 2011. http://iew.state.gov/

Institute of International Education, Inc. "Institute of International Education." Accessed April 12, 2011. http://www.iie.org/

Chapter 1
Knowing Their Background First: Understanding Prior Library Experiences Of International Students

John Hickok

This case study—by California State University Fullerton librarian John Hickok—describes how understanding the prior library experiences of international students, in their home countries, can be of tremendous help when instructing them on U.S. academic libraries' resources and services. The resources and services of libraries in other countries can vary dramatically from U.S. libraries; thus, a disconnect in understanding and using U.S. libraries can often result for international students. Librarians can help bridge this disconnect by learning about libraries of other countries. This can be done several ways: visiting foreign libraries, establishing overseas library partnerships, interviewing foreign faculty/staff, and interviewing international students themselves. Hickok describes how librarians—once prior library experiences of international students are identified—can better explain similarities and differences, thereby ensuring more effective library use.

Introduction

In this case study I will describe how learning about the home library conditions and prior library experiences of international students—before proceeding with library orientations or instruction sessions—can be of tremendous help when instructing them on U.S. academic libraries' resources and services. First, I will note the problem regarding international students and U.S. libraries, and what the professional library literature offers. Next, I will describe efforts I took to learn about international students' home library conditions. And finally, I will describe how I put this into action while instructing international students at my university. The hope is that this case study may be repeated or adapted by other academic librarians for their own international student populations.

The Institution

This case study occurred—and is currently ongoing—at California State University Fullerton (CSUF), a university of the 23-campus public, state university system of California, located in Fullerton (Orange County), California. CSUF's student population is ethnically diverse; 31% White, 30% Hispanic/Latino, 21% Asian (California State University Fullerton 2010). International students comprise almost 5% of the student population (1,660 students), with the majority from Asian countries (not surprising, as California is part of the Pacific Rim, and has the largest number of Asian-heritage residents in the U.S.) (U.S. Census Bureau 2010).

The Problem

As the Outreach Librarian to international students at California State University Fullerton (CSUF), I have been instructing international students on research and library skills for over twelve years. During this time, I have observed that international students' prior experiences with libraries in their home countries shape their perceptions and use of libraries while in the United States. Certainly the same can be said for U.S. domestic students—early library experiences while growing up shape their later perceptions and usage. However, the effect is more pronounced with international students. For example, international students growing up with libraries that are extremely limited in resources may arrive in the U.S. with a mind-set that libraries aren't useful. Or students growing up in countries where librarians are low-status clerks, rather than highly trained professionals, may arrive with a mind-set that librarians "don't know much." These mind-sets (or *schema*, to use an educational term), formed by their own first-hand experience, have serious implications when they arrive in the U.S. and are suddenly faced with assignments demanding library use and research skills.

Library Literature

The literature of the library profession covers the topic of international students in U.S. libraries extensively. From 2008-2010, I served as a compiler on this very topic for the ACRL Instruction Section's *Library Instruction for Diverse Populations Bibliography (*Association of College & Research Libraries 2008, currently available online). I read and annotated dozens of articles and book chapters addressing the topic of library instruction to international students. Some focused on the challenges international students face, such as English proficiency struggles (being unfamiliar with library jargon like "Call Number" or "Circulation"), as noted by Howzc and Moore (2003), and Curry and Copeman (2005), or cultural struggles (being uncomfortable with face-to-face interaction with a librarian), as noted by Jiao and Onwuebguzie (2001), and Gilton (2005).

Other authors focused on case studies or surveys to address international students' skills or needs—such as Wang (2008); Sackers, Secomb, and Hulett (2008); Liao, Finn, and Jun (2007); and Morrissey and Given (2006)—while still others offered case studies for specific projects about international student library instruction, like Macdonald (2008) and Hurley, Hegarty, and Bolger (2006). Similarly, Mu (2007), and Mundava and Gray (2008) offered suggestions on marketing library instruction and services to international students.

A few authors zeroed-in on international students' library experiences and library conditions from their home countries. Jackson (2005) discussed a survey given to newly-arrived international students on their prior library experience and opinions about libraries. Likewise, I did so, in a previous work on innovative strategies for library instruction to ESL/international students (Hickok 2008). Closely related, Overall (2009) noted the need for a "cultural competence framework" among librarians to better understand international students, and Ye (2009) argued that library literature too often treats international students as a single, homogenous population, when in fact, students' characteristics and background experiences vary dramatically from country to country.

The Initiative: Efforts to Learn about Students' Home Libraries

Having identified a problem and reviewed the literature, I realized I needed to better understand international students' home library conditions in order to understand the library perceptions with which they were arriving. There were several ways I went about doing this.

Visiting Foreign Libraries

Admittedly, visiting foreign libraries to learn about them is not exactly an economically feasible option; travel costs, especially to distant countries, are prohibitive. However, there is truth to the maxim "where there's a will there's a way." In 2005 I was eligible for sabbatical release time, so I wrote a research/travel grant proposal to investigate libraries in East & Southeast Asia—the region generating the majority of CSUF's international students. Because of the appeal of the proposal—to better serve international students—the grant was awarded. So for the entire 2005-6 school year, I lived in Asia, rotating each month among all 14 countries of the region, visiting, in total, over 200 libraries. Certainly, if I had not received release time and funding, I would not have been able to start at this scale. But I would have still started somehow; perhaps just a two-week or summer trip to one country only. To consider traveling, consult your institution's international office to determine the countries of greatest enrollment. Since dual-purpose trips are often easier to fund, inquire if there are existing trips organized by others (faculty, recruiters, etc.) with which you could travel.

The data I collected on the library conditions of all 14 countries is too voluminous to fit in this chapter, but I can give some examples, from five countries.

Indonesia. Indonesian libraries have made tremendous progress in recent years toward modernization. However, with the exception of top academic libraries, Indonesia still struggles to provide professionally-trained librarians. Thus, many "librarians" have no formal training, and, unfortunately, lead to the stereotype that librarians are more clerical caretakers than professional information experts. This situation often influences Indonesian students, who, upon arriving in the U.S. to study, may see no value in consulting U.S. reference librarians for research projects.

Vietnam. Vietnam has likewise made phenomenal progress in recent years toward modernization. Vietnam's top universities are now enjoying resource-rich databases similar to those in the U.S. However, for smaller and provincial universities and schools, resources—and especially e-resources—are much more limited or even nonexistent. Students, therefore, turn almost exclusively to the Internet (Google, etc.) for information-seeking. This condition leaves an experiential stamp on many Vietnamese students, such that if they study abroad to the U.S., their thinking is "Internet only" rather than library, for research.

China. China, as well, has made incredible library progress in recent years. I observed repeated construction of enormous library buildings on many university campuses. Internet and e-resources are plentiful at top university libraries. Modernization is underway at a dizzying pace—yet at the same time, some old scenarios persist. Several academic libraries still have closed stacks of general collections (paged by staff members only), and loan quantities are often still limited (e.g., 3–4 books maximum). These conditions, then, shape many Chinese students' perceptions, such that when in the U.S., they don't realize that they can openly browse through shelves and that loan quantities are much, much higher (students from China often stare at me in disbelief when I tell them how many CSUF library books they can take home!)

Korea. South Korea, as a highly developed country, already enjoys very modernized libraries. In fact, many of the university libraries I visited had high-tech innovations that even surpassed many U.S. academic libraries—like waving mobile phones over sensors to automatically enter student ID information for reserving study rooms. But a challenge for Korean libraries is making libraries—as material repositories—relevant. Many students I interviewed in Korean libraries were only in the library to study for standardized examinations, and had no experience using any of the materials. This experience affects those Korean students, who, once in the U.S., are faced with expectations from professors to find scholarly materials in the library.

Philippines. The Philippines has a strong library presence. Librarians were "professionalized" in 1990 (i.e., bachelors degree and licensure examination required), so trained librarians are more widespread. An interesting condition in Philippine academic libraries is the widespread use of student theses. Perhaps because expensive scholarly materials are not as available, student theses are amassed in libraries and heavily used as sources for undergraduate papers. Filipino students who come to the U.S. have to adjust to new expectations: scholarly publications over student theses.

Thus, by traveling to Asia—to the home countries and libraries of so many international students at CSUF—I gained invaluable firsthand insights into the conditions of, and attitudes toward, libraries and librarians there.

Establishing Overseas Library Partnerships

In addition to actually visiting libraries in other countries, I began establishing virtual partnerships with overseas libraries. Often this simply entailed a regular email exchange of information. I would email questions about their library conditions and services, and in exchange, they would email me questions about my library's activities. An example is Iran. I have never been to Iran, but began email communication with an academic librarian in Iran after meeting at an international conference in Malaysia. CSUF does not have many Iranian international students, but the insights I gained on Iran's libraries—from simple emails—gave me a better understanding when instructing Iranian international students.

To consider establishing overseas partnerships, once again consult your institution's international office to determine the countries of greatest enrollment, and if any formal exchanges or partnerships exist (if so, there is already a basis for communication!). The libraries of those foreign universities sending large numbers of international students can also be contacted. ALA's International Relations Roundtable also maintains a "Sister Library" website for matching U.S. and foreign libraries (American Library Association 2010).

Interviewing Foreign Faculty/Staff

Interviewing foreign faculty/staff at CSUF—whether visiting scholars, or previously immigrated—was another measure I took. Visiting scholars were especially useful, as they provided the freshest observations from their home countries. These interviews were not formal, scholarly interviews, but rather, casual conversations. I would email visiting scholars and offer to show them library resources supporting their research, and then afterwards, chat with them about libraries in their country. Sometimes it was even over coffee on campus. For example, in talking with a visiting professor from Fudan University in China, I gained further insights into the perception of librarians there (improving, but still low status). Immigrant faculty/staff were helpful too, but only if having immigrated within the past ten years; any longer than that posed a problem with the currency of their observations.

Interviewing International Students Themselves

This is by far the best approach. Here I am referring to real, face-to-face, Q&A interviews, not just impersonal surveys where just "checking a box" prevents more nuanced answers. By actually talking with international students about their experiences with libraries in their home countries, you gain the greatest insights. You can also recognize the error of stereotyping. While commonalities can be seen (for example, the heavy standardized testing in Korea and Japan, and libraries often used as study halls more than research centers), concluding that *all* Korean/Japanese students therefore have little library usage is grossly inaccurate.

For the past twelve years, I have taken the opportunity to interview international students during new student orientation. My component of their orientation (which is a presentation and tour) gives me the opportunity to solicit library experiences they've had, and compare those with the library conditions before them. For example, I have not yet traveled to India, but interviews with Indian international students have given me insights into the types of, and conditions of, libraries there.

Putting it into Action: Instructing Students

Armed with a greater awareness of students' home library conditions, I felt better prepared to understand international students while teaching them all the library has to offer. But beyond catching them at optional, professor-requested instruction sessions, how could I outreach to international students, specifically? Here, I took lessons from the literature—specifically the marketing articles by Mu and Mundava & Gray (noted earlier). Mundava & Gray's work—entitled "Meeting Them Where They Are"—advocated a proactive, outreach approach, by *going to* venues where international students gathered, such as student cultural clubs, international office activities, ESL classes, or departments with large international enrollments (e.g., Engineering, Business, etc.). This is exactly what I did.

Student Cultural Clubs

Each semester, CSUF hosts an outdoor fair of student clubs. I approached student cultural clubs, chatted with their officers, shared my interest in (or communication with, or travels to) their home countries, and proposed a brief visit to their club meeting to tell their members more about the *exciting resources in the library on their country*. The emphasis is intentional. "A presentation about the library" equates as "boring" to many students, particularly if they have had negative library experiences previously. But a presentation on "exciting resources about your country in the library" sparks interest. This was exactly my approach. The following are accounts of my outreach visits to the Indonesian, Vietnamese, Chinese, and Filipino cultural clubs.

Indonesian. The Indonesian student club—called *Permias*—was delighted to have someone on campus who had actually visited their country meet with them. I began by bringing them Indonesian coco-nut cookies (purchased at an Asian market in a nearby city) and created a lively, informal environment in which to share stories about living in Indonesia. I then shared PowerPoint photos of Indonesia—and in particular, of me visiting libraries in Indonesia. We discussed the per-ception of librarians in Indonesia, and I drew contrasts of that to U.S. librarians—master-degreed and information experts. I concluded with the crescendo of my visit: showcasing resources in the library related to Indonesia (brief introductions to the online catalog for books and media, and databases for Indonesian-related reading like Indonesian newspaper articles on *Lexis-Nexis*). What a delight; the students said they were incredibly honored to have someone so interested in them and their culture.

Figure 1.1: Fun with the Indonesian student club

Vietnamese. The Vietnamese student club—or VSA, Vietnamese Students Association—was likewise delighted to have me meet with them. I followed the same format: I began by bringing Vietnamese wa-fer cookies (imported from Vietnam and bought in the "Little Saigon" area of Orange County) and had lively discussions on Vietnam and Vietnamese culture. I then shared my PowerPoint photos of Vietnam and my visits to Vietnamese libraries. I used this opportunity to talk about library resources (or the lack of resources), comparing Internet Cafés in Vietnam to academic databases in CSUF's library. With photo-comparisons that were contextually-rich—e.g., a smaller library in Vietnam with only the Internet compared to the variety of databases in CSUF's library—the students better realized the resources available to them.

Figure 1.2: A Vietnamese library

Chinese. The Chinese student club—or ACS, Association of Chinese Students—was similarly pleased to have me meet with them. Once again, I followed the same format: I began by bringing treats. To make it even more fun, I brought fortune cookies, and used them as a cross-cultural discussion point—how fortune cookies are a mostly Chinese-American product, and not common in China. I then shared PowerPoint photos of my visits to Chinese libraries. This proved lively, as students were happy to see photos of universities they had attended. Here I noted similarities and differences, such as the closed vs. open collections and quantity limits on borrowing. The comparisons were effective, as several students expressed interest in "borrowing a *lot* more books." I then followed with showing the many Chinese-related the materials library owned: books, media, periodicals, databases, and more.

Figure 1.3: Fortune cookies for the Chinese Student club

Pilipino. I also met with the Pilipino American Student Association, or PASA. Most of the students were Pilipino-American, born or
raised in the U.S. But that didn't matter; the goal remained the same:
share with them about their country-of-heritage, and encourage them
to use the library. Snacks were again provided, and lively (Pilipino!)
music accompanied the slides of Philippine libraries. One particular
slide caused awe—of me personally holding a 100-year old diary page

Figure 1.4: A smaller Philippine library

of José Rizal (the Philippines' independence martyr and national hero) from a university archive I visited. Slides of smaller university libraries with fewer resources, caused an appreciation among PASA students for the resources available in CSUF's library.

One might argue, "these presentations were easy for you since you traveled to those locations; but what about for those of us who haven't?" Travel is not necessary for effective outreach presentations. I met with another campus cultural club—the South Pacific Islander Cultural Association, or SPICA—although I have never traveled to the South Pacific. The approach was the same: I arrived at their club meeting with treats, we socialized about their cultures, and I shared with them PowerPoint slides on the wonderful Polynesian resources in the library. On this occasion, I even compiled a summary of the library's Polynesian resources in the form of a brochure.

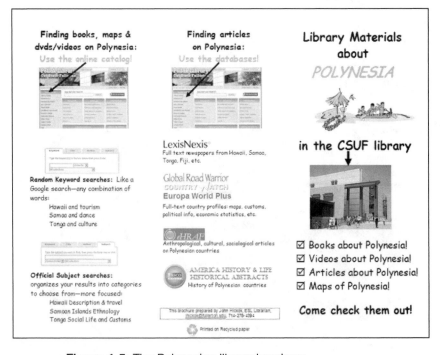

Figure 1.5: The Polynesian library brochure

International Office Activities

While not all international students participate in cultural clubs, all of them deal with the International Office. At CSUF, the International Office sponsors many activities: brown bag lunches, workshops, an honor society, and of course, the new student orientation. My share of the orientation—a library presentation and tour—is prime outreach time. It is during this time that I am able to interview them more personally, face to face (in small groups of about a dozen). In the technological wonderland of today, "walk-around" tours may seem, to some, an antiquated and time-wasting vestige of the past. "Why not just post photos or videos online for a virtual tour?" some have asked me. Certainly, those are options, and at CSUF's library, we have indeed used those. But relying on those alone fails to understand the power of experiential learning, especially for international students, when their concepts of libraries and librarians might be dramatically different.

When I conduct the walking tour with students, they receive a paper map/guide to the library and a 2-column comparison sheet of library resources/services in their country with those in the CSUF library. As similarities and differences are observed and experienced firsthand, the "mind sets" students may have come with suddenly give way

Figure 1.6: Walking Library Tour

to a new understanding. One semester, a Vietnamese student shared a comment with me that exemplifies this perfectly: "Wow, I had no idea librarians specialized in subjects…and in *my* major, even!"

Comparison of your home country (university) library and CSUF's library

Home library◻   CSUF Library▧

Shelves
1. Open for browsing?
2. How are the books arranged?

Checking out books
1. How do you check out books?
2. How many can you take? (& for how long?)

Reference help
1. How friendly/helpful are the librarians?
2. When & where is help available?

Magazines/Newspapers/Journals
1. Where are they? Are there many?
2. Can you photocopy them? Take them home?

Library Catalog
1. Is the catalog electronic (online)?
2. Is it accessible outside the library?
3. How do you look up a book?

Databases
1. What kind of article databases are there?
2. Are they accessible outside the library?
3. How do you look up an article?

Figure 1.7: 2-column comparison sheet

ESL Classes

ESL classes are another key venue for reaching out to international students. At CSUF, nearly 200 international students take pre-admission ESL classes (called the American Language Program) to pass the TOEFL English entrance exam. ESL instructors have been wonderful partners, as they know the importance of the library once these students matriculate into the university. As a result, I have visited many ESL classes to conduct similar outreach activities, employing the same techniques: a lively, informal setting with a conversational exchange of students' prior library experiences, and tours with comparison sheets.

While ESL classes are usually a mix of nationalities, sometimes-large cohorts of students from a single country arrive. This gives me the opportunity to zero-in on their country's libraries, with country-specific presentations. Such was the case with a large group of students from Korea. I was able to directly relate with them by talking about libraries at "their" universities, all in a jovial, informal setting (complete with popcorn!).

Departments with Large International Enrollments

Departments with large international enrollments are also smart to target. For example, at CSUF the engineering departments (civil, mechanical, electrical) have a high enrollment of Middle Eastern international students. Departments often have departmental societies, or departmental student associations, with regular meeting times. Student officers could be approached, just as I did with cultural club officers, with the offer to stop by for a presentation. Department chairs could also be approached, and asked in which engineering courses a brief library presentation—directly in the classroom, to pose less interruption for the professor—might be acceptable.

This type of outreach I have not yet initiated; however, plans are being made! I am already consulting Middle Eastern and engineering resources in the library, to create an enticing PowerPoint presentation.

Conclusion

As both my own experience and the professional literature has shown, realizing the similarities and differences between U.S. and other countries' libraries—by both U.S. librarians and the international students—adds to better learning and understanding of the library. The disconnect between international students' view of libraries/librarians—and what actually exists before them in the U.S.—can be significant. But proactive strategies, as discussed in this chapter, can make a difference. At the end of a week, or a month, or even a semester, if I have helped an international student understand that they need scholarly sources for their research, that the library has such sources via databases or its collections, and that librarians are expert information professionals there to assist them, then I have done an effective job of outreach. It is a doable, repeatable and adaptable approach, and one from which all academic libraries with international student populations can benefit.

References

American Library Association. International Relations Roundtable. 2010. "Sister Library Initiative." (August 2010). Accessed January 31, 2011. http://wikis.ala.org/sisterlibraries/index.php/Main_Page.

Association of College & Research Libraries. Instruction Section. 2008. "Library Instruction for Diverse Populations Bibliography." Accessed January 31, 2011. http://www.ala.org/ala/mgrps/divs/acrl/about/sections/is/projpubs/diversebib.cfm.

California State University Fullerton. Institutional Research and Analytical Studies. 2010. "Fall 2010 Ethnic Distributions." (Fall 2010). Accessed January 31, 2011. http://www.fullerton.edu/analyticalstudies/ethnicity/ethpie104.pdf.

Curry, Ann and Deborah Copeman. 2005. "Reference Service to International Students: A Field Stimulation Research Study." *The Journal of Academic Librarianship* 31 (5): 409–20.

Gilton, Donna L. 2005. "Culture Shock in the Library: Implications for Information Literacy Instruction." *Research Strategies* 20 (4): 424–32.

Hickok, John. 2008. "Bringing Them into the Community : Innovative Library Instructional Strategies for International and ESL Students." In *Practical Pedagogy for Library Instructors: 17 Innovative Strategies to Improve Student Learning*, edited by Douglas Cook and Ryan Sittler, 159–167. Chicago: Association of College and Research Libraries.

Howzc, Philip C. and Dorothy M. Moore. 2003. "Measuring International Students' Understanding of Concepts Related to the Use of Library-Based Technology." *Research Strategies* 19 (1): 57–74.

Hurley, Tina, Nora Hegarty, and Jennifer Bolger. 2006. "Crossing a Bridge: The Challenges of Developing and Delivering a Pilot Information Literacy Course for International Students." *New Library World* 107 (7/8): 302–320.

Jackson, Pamela. 2005. "Incoming International Students and the Library: A Survey." *Reference Services Review* 33 (2): 197–209.

Jiao, Qun G. and Anthony J. Onwuebguzie. 2001. "Sources of Library Anxiety Among International Students." *Urban Library Journal* 11 (1): 16–27.

Liao, Yan, Mary Finn, and Lu Jun. 2007. "Information-Seeking Behavior of International Graduate Students vs. American Graduate Students: A User Study at Virginia Tech 2005." *College & Research Libraries* 68 (1): 5–25.

Macdonald, Katrina. "ESL Library Skills: An Information Literacy Program for Adults with   Low Levels of English Literacy." *Australian Library Journal* 57 (3): 295–309.

Morrissey, Renée and Lisa M. Given. 2006. "International Students and the Academic Library: A Case Study." *Canadian Journal of Information & Library Sciences* 30 (¾): 221–239.

Mu, Cuiying. 2007. "Marketing Academic Library Resources and Information Services to International Students from Asia." *Reference Services Review* 35 (4):

571–83.

Mundava, Maud C. and LaVerne Gray. 2008. "Meeting Them Where They Are: Marketing to International Student Populations in U.S. Academic Libraries." *Technical Services Quarterly* 25 (3): 35–48.

Overall, Patricia M. 2009. "Cultural Competence: A Conceptual Framework for Library Information Science Professionals." *The Library Quarterly* 79 (2): 175–204.

Sackers, Nicole, Bess Secomb, and Heather Hulett. 2008. "How Well Do You Know Your Clients?: International Students' Preferences for Learning about Library Services." *Australian Academic & Research Libraries* 39 (1): 38–55.

U.S. Census Bureau. 2010. "Annual State Resident Population Estimates for 6 Race Groups by Age, Sex, and Hispanic Origin, April 1, 2000 to July 1, 2009." (June 2010). Accessed January 31, 2011. http://www.census.gov/compendia/statab/2011/tables/11s0019.pdf.

Wang, Jiannan. 2008. "Toward Understanding International Students: A Study Conducted at Middle Tennessee State University." *The Southeastern Librarian* 56 (3): 4–10.

Ye, Yunshan. 2009. "New Thoughts on Library Outreach to International Students." *Reference Services Review* 37 (1): 7–9.

Chapter 2
Chapter 2
Engaging International Students Before Welcome Week

Jannelle Ruswick

New international students come to campus with expectations of libraries that may be wildly different from the libraries at their new university. Libraries that wait until Welcome Week are missing prime opportunities to educate new international students about the ways they differ from libraries abroad. New international students' confusion and anxiety can be alleviated by extending outreach activities from the day they are admitted to the day they start their first class. This chapter describes orientation activities, online resources, and physical building changes that libraries can conduct before Welcome Week events commence.

Introduction

A common tradition in higher education is Welcome Week, where colleges and universities keep new students busy with parties, open houses, and informational events the week before classes start. The problem with Welcome Week is that it happens too late for international students who have already been here for a few weeks. United States Immigration and Customs Enforcement policies allow international students to arrive in the United States up to 30 days prior to the date listed on their I-20 forms, which is typically the first day of classes (U.S. Immigration and Customs Enforcement 2011). Many international students take advantage of this early entrance because it gives them more time to adjust to a new campus in a new city. This means international students may be here for a month, looking for ways to fill their days after decorating their dorm rooms and testing cafeteria food.

By the time Welcome Week arrives, hundreds of international students will have already been inside the library because it is one of the few university buildings open when classes are not in session. The early arrivers who enter the library become curious about how the library operates because they observe differences from their home libraries. In an effort to educate and prepare new international students, the Paul V. Galvin Library at the Illinois Institute of Technology decided to offer services and instruction for the 30 days prior to the start of classes. This chapter will explain how, through campus partnerships, programming, and building changes, we successfully equipped our new international students with library skills necessary to their success.

The Institution

The Illinois Institute of Technology is a private not-for-profit Ph.D. granting institution that specializes in science, technology, engineering and mathematics. The main campus is located in the historic Bronzeville neighborhood of Chicago, Illinois, with additional campuses in downtown Chicago, Wheaton, and Summit, Illinois. In the 2010–11 school year there were 7,774 students, of which forty percent (3,127 students) are international. Only twenty percent of international students are undergraduates; the remaining eighty percent are pursuing graduate or law degrees (Illinois Institute of Technology 2011). The main library is the Paul V. Galvin Library, where over half its patrons are international students. Galvin Library serves all students, but focuses on the colleges of engineering, science and letters, and psychology. There are separate libraries for architecture, graduate business, and law.

The Initiative

Gathering Information

Before deciding what types of services or activities to offer new international students it is important to have a good understanding of who they are and what they need. Effective methods of collecting this information include student population data, library patron counts, and a qualitative survey of current international students. Staff members in the international center, admissions, or institutional information can provide you with data about the number of international students at your institution and where they come from. Obtaining student ID numbers at designated times from the building entrance and online authentication system (e.g. EZ Proxy) will reveal to you if your user population is representative of the overall student population.

Galvin librarians wanted to see if the library user profile matched the student population profile. To determine this, we conducted an entrance count in the spring of 2009 using a sample size with a ninety-five percent confidence level and a confidence interval of plus or minus three. Online authentication data was obtained for the same time period. Our anecdotal evidence that most of our users were international students was accurate. We learned that fifty-eight percent of all student library users are international students, which is eighteen percent higher than the general university population. The breakdown between graduate and undergraduate international users was similar to the university's ratio, with eighty-three percent of our international students pursuing graduate degrees and seventeen percent seeking undergraduate degrees. The two most representative countries were China and India, which also aligned with the university's statistics. Discovering that most of our international users were graduate students was very informative in deciding on programming, as it meant that the incoming international students arrived with some prior academic library experience. Our knowledge of the various library systems in India and China also helped us be conscious that the students' previous library experience may have been very different from what they will experience here.

The third data gathering method was an optional qualitative survey of international students also conducted in the spring semester of 2009 to learn about the experiences of international students in libraries here and abroad. Surveys were disseminated in international student workshops and available online. Questions focused on many of our curiosities and assumptions about their prior libraries (see Appendix A for survey questions). What we learned from the responses helped us prioritize what information new international students needed so they could be prepared and feel confident about using Galvin Library. We determined that the major areas to focus on with new international students were the building's features and procedures, and the course reserve system. About half of our respondents said that their libraries at home gave them all their textbooks. Many respondents expressed curiosity about how our books are organized and why people were so noisy in the library. If students arrive with preconceptions about what a library is that vary widely from what we are, they will have trouble adapting. We hypothesized that teaching the incoming international students important tasks such as obtaining their textbooks and navigating the building before the semester began would relieve students' frustration and anxiety.

Building Changes and Staff Education

The surveys and demographic data gathered in the spring of 2009 helped the library staff see our building in a new light. To prepare for the next wave of incoming students we read all the signs and maps and observed study habits throughout the library. Our objective was to experience the building the way a new international student would. The most apparent area of confusion was in our presentation of building hours. New international students arrive during intersession, a time of reduced hours of operation between summer and fall classes. During this time we close at 5:00 p.m. and are not open on Sundays, so new students using the library tend to believe those are the regular building hours and could be disappointed in such limited hours of operation. If the students read any of the signs around the building they would see the phrase "summer intersession hours" which is confusing academic jargon. We remedied this in two ways. First, we changed the signs to say "summer hours," and below the current hours we included the "normal semester hours." Second, as we closed the building each day at 5:00 p.m. we would speak to each person and tell him or her that once school starts we have expanded hours. Reviewing building signage and editing them for simplicity and clarity is a great way to ensure the building is easy to navigate for new international students.

In addition to a comprehensive review of the building, staff participated in several training sessions and educational meetings in the winter of 2009/2010. The results of the surveys were explained at these meetings, and staff members were encouraged to discuss their experiences with new international students. Education on the different types of libraries around the world helped the staff gain a better understanding of our new students' sources of confusion. In these meetings we were able to establish which sources of confusion needed the most emphasis before school starts (such as clarifying our hours) as well as create ideas for outreach to new international students. These will be described in greater detail in the next section. The usefulness of these meetings has extended far beyond the period before Welcome Week because staff members continue to use the methods and information they learned throughout the year. Public services staff members participated in a refresher meeting in June of 2010. The purpose of the meeting was to remind staff of what they learned in the previous meetings, and talk about any changes in student behavior they observed since the last meeting. Staff also discussed methods of interpersonal communication they have found effective when working with our new international students, such as smiling frequently, adapting to the student's personal communication style, and avoiding slang. Immediately after the June meeting staff were able to put what they learned into practice with new international students who hadn't yet stepped inside the building.

Long Distance Engagement

Once a student commits to a university, the student gets excited and interested in all aspects of their new school. The incoming student will add the university to their list of schools on Facebook and order clothes adorned with the school's name. Librarians should not delay or ignore helping newly admitted students until they move in, especially in an era where the library is at their fingertips through the Internet. This initial excitement also gives the library a chance to capitalize on their interest and educate them. While it is easier and often accurate to respond to inquiries from incoming international students with "you must wait until you have arrived" or "trust me, you don't really need to use us yet," such responses come across as unfriendly and devalue the library's resources and services. Creating dedicated international student library Web pages and engaging in speedy and helpful virtual communication are two great ways to introduce new international students to the library.

Curious incoming international students have several introductory resources available to them through a dedicated section on our Web site. The international student section includes a LibGuide that international students can read prior to arriving: http://guides.library.iit.edu/internationalstudents. There is also a guide that explains the top nine differences between our library and common features of libraries in other countries. Another popular feature is a short virtual tour of the library that has been translated into five different languages: English, Chinese, Korean, Spanish and Hindi. Library student workers collaborated with librarians to translate the videos to ensure accuracy in language and meaning. The virtual tour is helpful because most international students do not visit IIT before enrolling. Most of the information, including the virtual tour, is heavily adapted from existing information, so the time and effort needed to create the section is not as daunting as it may seem. The international-specific context makes the international students aware that we understand them and are here to help.

Every spring and summer we get questions through instant messaging (IM) and email from newly admitted international students who want to use the library databases and e-books right away. In most cases the students have not registered for classes yet and therefore are not eligible for off-campus access to our resources. Instead of assuming they have not registered and giving the "wait until school starts" response, we take a minute to look up their student information and see if they have registered for classes. If the student is fully enrolled we can create their account to let them begin exploring our e-resources from home. The amount of additional time it takes to add a student ID number to the authentication database is minimal compared to the benefits of the student having a positive first library interaction and their ability to familiarize themselves with our resources. They see us as willing to go the extra mile to make sure they are satisfied, and they have time to learn about the library before they arrive.

Campus Partnerships

As with any library outreach project, cooperation with numerous departments across campus is crucial to the success of the project. Libraries cannot provide quality information and programming to incoming international students without the assistance of the International Center, Office of Admissions, and the Office of Student Affairs or their equivalents. Student support departments can sometimes fail to see how libraries are important to the initial success of a new student, so it is the library's responsibility to enlighten them. Taking advantage of any pre-existing personal connections is an easy way to start. Some non-academic departments ask the library to help them find data or conduct basic research, but are not aware of how much interaction library staff have with the student population. Librarians who know people in these departments should talk to their connections about the issues facing new international students and how the library fits in to their acclimatization. For departments where there is no pre-existing bond, a phone call or in-person conversation forges a deeper connection than introductory emails to unknown contacts.

Our relationship with the International Center has been essential in building awareness and credibility with incoming international students. After conducting our surveys (see Appendices A and B) we met with staff from the International Center to show them our findings and discuss the ways we are important to the international student's overall experience at the university. From the International Center we were able to get a detailed timeline of when students arrive and what tasks they must complete upon arrival. For example, we learned that international students must check in with the International Center as soon as they arrive on campus. With this knowledge we were able to create promotional materials that the Center's staff gave to the new students when they checked in. Our strong relationship also allows us to coordinate workshop times to avoid scheduling conflicts and to reach the international students via the International Center's mailing list. The library and the International Center are now involved in joint ventures such as co-teaching workshops for international students and creating online guides.

Our relationship with the Office of Admissions has resulted in the library having a table at all admissions events and prospective student open houses. This gives us a chance to promote the library to students before they choose to attend IIT. While open houses are useful, international students do not typically attend them. However, remaining on the Admission's office schedule helps remind them to include us on international events as well. Admissions staff also updates us with enrollment counts. This data helps us determine how many introductory library workshops to offer. It also lets us know which majors are popular among the incoming students, which informs decisions in all library functions from collections to instruction. For example, if we know 200 new international students are going to major in electrical engineering, we can begin working with the electrical engineering department to assist in research training for their students.

The department that has given us the most access to new students is the Office of Student Affairs, which is in charge of new student orientations, in addition to all student organizations and social events. We developed a long-term partnership with the Office of Student Affairs by serving on the summer orientation committee, which includes representatives from across the university. The wide reach of the committee helped the library promote our services to people with whom we previously had little to no relationship. It also helped strengthen bonds with representatives from the International Center and the Center for Diversity and Inclusion. We volunteered to coordinate other portions of the two-day orientation, in addition to the library segment. Offering to assist with non-library-related orientation functions showcased the library staff's talent. We forged several new connections by showing departments all across campus that the library is cooperative, savvy, and helpful.

New Student Orientations

Incoming freshman orientations are a common event at many universities. Depending on the size of the school, these orientations can have hundreds of new students attend; often too many to fit into a library. This leaves the library stuck speaking to the students in a large auditorium, or worse, not having any involvement. For libraries fortunate enough to get a part in orientation, there are several guidelines that should be used when presenting to any student group, but particularly to international student groups: keep the message simple, use engaging presentation methods, and concentrate on what they want to know versus what we want to tell them. For example, instead of touting the large number of journal subscriptions, talk about favorite study spots in the building. Experiment with software other than PowerPoint for visuals, speak from personal experience, and get out from behind the podium to connect with your audience. It is important not to overwhelm the attendees with information, so limit the presentation to only the things they need to know to succeed in their first few weeks of the semester. While some may argue that this doesn't teach them everything they need to know about the library, this is not the point of an orientation and not what they are looking for. This "what you need to know now" alleviates library anxiety for new international students because they feel prepared to perform immediately necessary tasks.

At IIT, student orientations are two-day events held throughout June and July. Students and parents spend the time learning about campus, socializing, and registering for classes. International students are typically unable to attend these sessions, so the orientation schedule includes a special orientation session in August intended primarily for international students. The special session premiered in August 2009, and the summer orientation committee was looking for ways to fill the schedule. We had shown in previous orientations that the library offered informative and entertaining programming, and were given forty-five minutes after their mandatory immigration regulations session. Although our portion was listed as optional in the schedule it occurred in the same building as the previous session, so students could be funneled right into our program. We had promotional signs and a librarian outside their mandatory session to help direct people to the right room. Around fifty students attended, which was about a quarter of the overall orientation attendance. A benefit of the session being in August, versus June or July like other sessions, was that school started the next week. This meant that instead of simply mentioning we have textbooks on reserve, we could show them how to search for their textbooks in the catalog.

Much of the forty-five minute session was devoted to the two areas of known confusion: textbooks and the library building. Our surveys showed an overwhelming number of students were confused about where to get their textbooks, and procuring textbooks is one of the first things students take care of. Many international students come from systems where the library loans every student all of their textbooks for the duration of the semester, so they are shocked, stressed and frustrated when they learn that we do not perform the same service. In the presentation, we focused on the rationale behind our textbook policy, how the course reserve system works, and how to search the catalog for specific titles. We also explained how to buy textbooks, since this is a new task to many of the students. Discussing checking out textbooks gave us an opportunity to explain call numbers, which is another area of confusion for new international students. The rest of the session focused on the hours we are open, and discussed some building aspects that may be new to them such as being able to talk and eat throughout the library.

In the summer of 2010 we had a different set-up for the August international student orientation. We were given thirty minutes in a large auditorium, and this time our program was not listed as optional. There were about 200 students and a few parents in attendance. A few students were domestic students who were unable to attend a June or July session, but mostly the participants were international. The focus was the same as the previous year's presentation, where we explained things they need to know to be ready for the first week of classes. The library was scheduled for three o'clock. After hours of shuffling around campus to listen to other speakers, their minds were numb from too many PowerPoint presentations. We wanted to be a refreshing change to their day that would result in a lasting impression. To help foster a positive reaction, we used Prezi, a free online presentation generator that functions like a giant pin-up board where the screen bounces around the board in a pre-designated path. From the moment the students filed in we noticed that the audience was intrigued by the atypical presentation on the screen (view the presentation at http://prezi.com/y3ylbf_onix9/galvin-library/). Prezi kept the students' interest because they were curious to see what was going to happen next. The screen never had more than a photo or a few words on it, which complimented the speaker without being too distracting. Afterwards, several students came up to the podium to ask how the "slides" were made and complimented the speaker's casual style.

The key to these large auditorium presentations is to make the audience feel like they have learned a lot about the library while covertly instilling a sense of urgency in the students to learn more before classes begin. We wanted them to know we are a popular, friendly place that has the resources they need to succeed. We also wanted them to know that we didn't even scratch the surface during the presentation and that in order to be truly prepared they needed to attend our in-house orientations the next day. If the students believed they learned everything they needed to know at the presentation, they would be less inclined to come to the library the next day for a far more informative and personal library introduction.

In-House Orientations

Regardless of the level of involvement in campus-wide orientation activities, libraries should offer their own in-house orientations and tours to international students. The number of incoming international students should dictate the number of sessions to offer. In addition to sessions occurring during or immediately after campus-wide orientations, sessions should also be offered throughout the thirty-day period prior to the first day of classes. The early sessions give the students more time to adjust to the library. It is important to ensure that the times do not conflict with any other events on campus. Using admissions numbers helps determine the appropriate number of sessions. Too many sessions can lead to a class where only one person attends, which leaves the attendee feeling self-conscious for being the only person in his peer group to be there. Reaching a critical mass of students increases interest and involvement during the session. Promotional activities are simple since the audience is so targeted. Fliers can be given to the students as part of their International Center check-in packet. Hang a few of the same fliers around the library, and encourage any new international student you meet to attend.

Galvin Library had special orientation sessions for international students for a few years before the official orientation committee began their dedicated international student session in 2009. We piloted our "Library Fundamentals for New International Students" sessions in January 2007 because fewer new students are admitted for the spring semester. In the inaugural year, the sessions were offered at eleven and one o'clock the day after new student orientation for all students (where we had only five minutes to speak wedged between other departments). We had an additional session at the end of the first week of class. Library Fundamentals for New International Students is not a very flashy or creative title, but it uses terminology familiar to the students and conveys the purpose of the session. We experimented with other titles such as "Introduction to the Library for New International Students," but the word introduction gave the impression that the sessions would be too general to make them worth attending. Ultimately the name is not a huge issue, as the students learned about the session during orientation and the fliers detailed the sessions' content (see Appendix B for sample flier).

Library classrooms with Internet access and projection screens are the optimal setting for new student sessions. Having a prepared presentation with presentation software such as PowerPoint is helpful for many reasons. Non-native English speakers will appreciate the ability to hear and read the information simultaneously. The students can take notes that will have contextual support when they refer to them in the future. Also, including screenshots in the PowerPoint slides allow the students to remember specific steps of a library task. Whenever a live demonstration is necessary, such as doing a catalog search, skip over the screenshots and perform the task live. Skipping between the PowerPoint and live demonstrations helps break up the monotony of a scripted presentation.

Our sessions occur in either the Library Learning Center or a conference room. The Library Learning Center has computers in it, but we don't use them during the sessions for a few reasons. We regularly have standing room only attendance at these sessions, so trying to get students to perform tasks throughout the presentation was difficult to coordinate and time-consuming. Sessions are slowed considerably if the librarian has to spend a lot of time fixing broken computers or assisting students who clicked on the wrong link and are lost. Also, nearly all of our attendees are graduate students who understand the importance of learning about the library and can pay attention without having to follow along on a computer. The conference room has a flat screen television to display the presentation, and the students can sit in more relaxed clusters versus rows of computers. The conference room also eliminates potential distractions and poor sight lines as a result of computer monitors. We decorate the rooms with welcome banners and balloons to make the space look more festive.

As students enter the classroom they are welcomed, asked for their names and where they are from, and are asked to complete a brief survey. The librarian explains that the survey answers will help her know what to focus on during class. Directions and questions on the survey should be brief and written with non-native English speakers in mind. There should also be room for the student to write a question they would like answered during the session. Scanning the responses before presenting helps the librarian know how much time to devote to a particular topic.

The first year we conducted these sessions, we discovered the importance of clear and simple survey instructions. The students were asked to answer yes or no to statements about their previous library experience and to circle library terms they did not understand, such as catalog. This design was too confusing and complicated. Students were providing inconclusive answers by circling entire sentences that they would say yes to, or only circling words but not providing a yes or no answer. We have since removed the jargon-circling instruction and just have the students answer yes or no to the statements, which has reduced confusion considerably (see Appendix C for survey example). The attendees have always appreciated that librarians take a moment to look over the survey responses and questions before the presentation begins. The students were able to avoid apprehension about raising their hands or asking a question during the presentation because we already had their questions in front of us. The students felt that the session was customized for their needs, and that we would definitely discuss what they wanted to know.

The first semester we held these sessions we did not give a library tour as part of the session. We wanted to market the session as a quick introduction, and incorrectly thought that a tour wasn't necessary since the building is only two floors. We added a tour component the next semester after one of our interns, an international student herself, said that the building tour is extremely important to international students. The tour ended up being a wonderful way to demonstrate new concepts such as the Library of Congress classification system, how to log on to computers, how to get a copy card, and other common tasks. Our tour includes stops at the circulation and reference desks where the staff members there say hello and describe what they do for the students. This alleviates confusion as to where the student should go in the future, and lets them know that professional librarians are here to help them with their research.

Student Resource Fairs

Libraries that do not have the resources or time to prepare for large-scale orientation sessions can still reach incoming international students. Having a table at a student resource fair or open house takes almost no preparation. Find out if and when your university offers such events and ask for a table. In our experience resource fair coordinators are happy to give the library a table; the more participants the better. Bring a few handouts that you believe would be most immediately useful to your students, such as a library checklist of tasks to complete during their first month at school (see Appendix D for checklist example). All that is left is to have a few outgoing librarians sit at the table, encourage students to stop and chat, and answer questions. Resource fairs are a great way to showcase the helpfulness and approachability of librarians.

Since August 2009, there have been two resource fairs on the schedule of the international orientation session: the Student Resource Fair and the Community Resource Fair. Both fairs happen on the second day of orientation. The Student Resource Fair occurs in the morning while the Community Resource Fair is in the late afternoon. We spoke to the students in the auditorium the previous day, so they already had some knowledge about the library. We have traditionally only attended the Student Resource Fair, where participants from campus departments ranging from the library to food services to Greek organizations speak about their services. Students go to the fair while they wait for their advising appointment. Having the fair occur the day after they heard our presentation has been very helpful because they can ask us questions about what we told them the previous day. We have two librarians sit at the table with no specific agenda other than to answer questions and introduce themselves.

Later in the afternoon the Community Resource Fair occurs. The difference between this and the Student Resource Fair is that the Community Resource Fair features non-school related participants. Students take care of important functions such as signing up for cell phone plans and creating bank accounts at this fair. In the 2010 August international student orientation, we asked if we could have a table at this fair in an effort to increase awareness among international students. Unlike the Student Resource Fair where we let the students guide the conversation, our goal for this fair was to educate the students specifically about how to create their online library accounts. Our rationale was that they were signing up for accounts for other services, so they could also create their library accounts during the fair.

We had mixed results with our time at the Community Resource Fair. This fair is extremely important to the international students, so nearly all new international students attend. By attending this fair we maximized the number of opportunities for student interaction. However, we believe the additional three hours of one on one time with the students hurt our attendance at the Library Fundamentals for New International Students workshops held the next day, as those sessions had record low attendance. Nothing in our planning of these sessions was different from the previous successful years. Our theory for the reason behind the low attendance is that students felt that they had all their questions answered at the fairs, so they didn't need to attend our sessions the next day.

Library Socials and Parties

The pre-Welcome Week events for our new international students are fairly formal. There are a few reasons we have decided to avoid the nontraditional events popular at other libraries like gaming or casino nights. While it is important to have targeted events to meet the informational needs of international students, we would not want to have a party that was exclusionary. We have no budget for food, decorations, or supplies, so a fun event that the entire campus was invited to would be impossible to pull off. Also, our international student population is mostly composed of graduate students who do not require a party to show them the importance of the library. They are here to study complex subjects in the sciences and engineering, and they already know they will need the library to succeed. This means that we do not need to market the library to get them to use it; instead, we need to explain how the library works so that they may best make use of it. Knowing your students makes all the difference when deciding whether to offer social events as part of your pre-Welcome Week activities for new international students.

Conclusion

The result of all of our efforts at campus orientations, Library Fundamentals sessions, resource fairs, online communications, and Web pages have had a noticeably positive effect on the acclimation of new international students in the library. There are fewer new international students coming to the library the first week of classes unaware of our textbook policies as there were before we began our outreach efforts. By the time school starts most international students have met several staff members or seen a librarian speak. Librarians who present to new international students have remarked that they will have attendees seek them out throughout the semester saying "I saw you talk at orientation, and I have a question." Connections made before school have helped the international students feel comfortable approaching librarians when they need help.

Another positive effect of our hard work is that the university administration recognized the library's importance in the lives of international students by approving a new full time librarian position dedicated to serving the international population. The first International Student Library Services Liaison began employment in October 2010, and is in charge of the activities discussed in this chapter. The position is similar to being the library liaison for a campus department, but the "department" in this case is a specific student population. As a liaison, the librarian ensures that international students' perspectives are considered and their needs are met in all areas of public services. She conducts library instruction in both English and Mandarin Chinese that introduces the research process to international students, creates multilingual online tutorials and LibGuides, and educates campus staff and faculty on the difficulties international students may have when researching. This position has broadened our capacity to help international students acclimate, learn and succeed at an American university.

The activities described in this chapter did not require any special funding to complete. All that a library needs to conduct similar pre-Welcome Week events are a few outgoing librarians and copies of fliers and handouts. After the creation of the various workshops, presentations, and handouts, only minor edits from one year to the next is necessary. As more international students come to the United States to study, the demand for pre-Welcome Week library services and activities increasingly important. New international students have enough to worry about. Remove the library from that list of worries and watch as they develop into savvy library users from the start.

References

Illinois Institute of Technology. 2011. "IIT Quick Facts." Last modified January 05, 2011. http://www.iit.edu/about/quick_facts.shtml.

U.S. Immigration and Customs Enforcement. 2011. "Fact Sheet: Arriving at a U.S. Port of Entry...What a Student Can Expect." Accessed January 20, 2011. http://www.ice.gov/sevis/factsheet/100104ent_stdnt_fs.htm.

Appendix A: Qualitative Survey Questions

The questions on this page will ask you about the features of your last school library. We will use the responses to increase our understanding of international students' library experiences.

1. Did you use any of the following libraries in your native country? (select all that apply)
   - ☐ Secondary school library (high school, gymnasia, preparatory school, etc)
   - ☐ College or university library
   - ☐ Private research library
   - ☐ Public library
   - ☐ Other (please specify)

2. How often did you use your last library?
   - ☐ Never (skip to the next page if you selected never)
   - ☐ A few times a semester
   - ☐ A few times a month
   - ☐ A few times a week
   - ☐ Every day

3. Did your library allow you to borrow textbooks?
   - ☐ No, the library did not have textbooks available.
   - ☐ Yes, the library let me read them inside the library for a certain amount of time. I could not take them out of the building.
   - ☐ Yes, the library gave me all of my textbooks at the start of each semester.
   - ☐ Other (please specify)

4. Did your library offer classes on how to use the library?
   - ☐ Yes   ☐ No
   - ☐ Do not know

5. Did your library have librarians who were available to help you with your library research?
❑ Yes   ❑ No
❑ Do not know

6. Did your library provide access to databases and electronic resources from off-campus (home, work, coffee shop, etc)?
❑ Yes   ❑ No
❑ Do not know

7. Overall, how satisfied were you with your last library?
❑ Extremely satisfied
❑ Very satisfied
❑ Satisfied
❑ Not very satisfied
❑ Very dissatisfied

Please answer these brief questions if you have used Galvin Library before. If you are new to IIT, you may skip to the next page.

8. How often do you go to Galvin Library?
❑ Never
❑ A few times a semester
❑ A few times a month
❑ A few times a week
❑ Every day

9. What do you do when you go to Galvin Library? (select all that apply)
❑ Study in groups
❑ Study alone
❑ Browse the books, newspapers, and journals on the shelves
❑ Use the Internet for personal use
❑ Take a break between classes Ask a librarian a question
❑ Attend a library class or workshop

❑ Use textbooks on reserve
❑ Check out books
❑ Use the Internet for academic purposes
❑ Other (please specify)

10. How often do you use the library's website, databases, and electronic resources from anywhere outside of Galvin (home, office, etc.)?
❑ Never
❑ A few times a semester
❑ A few times a month
❑ A few times a week
❑ Every day

11. What services would you like to see the library provide?
12. What materials would you like to see the library provide?
13. Do you find anything confusing about the library? If yes, describe it here.

Please provide a bit of information about yourself. This information is confidential and will be used to categorize responses.

14. What is your IIT status?
❑ Graduate student   ❑ Undergraduate student
❑ Other

15. Are you male or female?
❑ Male   ❑ Female

16. How old are you?
❑ Under 18 years old
❑ 18–21 years old
❑ 22–28 years old
❑ 28–36 years old
❑ 36 years old or older

17. What is your country of origin and what languages (other than English) do you speak?
    ☐ Country of origin
    ☐ Languages spoken

Thank you for participating in our survey! If you want to be eligible for a $25 iTunes gift card, please enter your IIT email address here. Email addresses are not attached to your survey answers and are confidential.

18. IIT email address:

Appendix B: Library Fundamentals for New International Students Promotional Flier

Top 10 questions new international students have about Galvin Library...

1. Where are my textbooks?
2. When is the library open?
3. How are the books organized?
4. How many books can I take home?
5. Do you have any e-books?

6. Can I talk in the library?
7. How do I request a book?
8. What is my log in information?
9. How is Galvin Library different from my old library?
10. I'm confused! Who can help me?

In less than one hour
Fundamentals for New International Students
Will answer these questions and take you on a full tour!

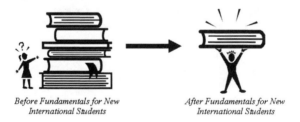

Before Fundamentals for New
International Students

After Fundamentals for New
International Students

Come to any one of these 7 sessions:
Friday, August 13 at 2 pm
Tuesday, August 17 at 3 pm
Friday, August 20 at 10 am, 1 pm and 3 pm
Tuesday, August 31 at 10 am and 12:50 pm

Register at http://galvinlibrary.wordpress.com
Each session will cover the same material, so you only need to attend one session.

Appendix C: Survey of Past Library Experiences

Welcome to Paul V. Galvin Library!

Please complete this short survey so we can best assist you today.

What is your major? _____

Where are you from? _____

What languages do you speak? _____

1. Circle yes or no to each of the following statements:

My library at home let me find books on the shelves by myself. Yes or No

My library at home gave me all my textbooks at the start of each semester. Yes or No

My library at home let me check out books and take them home. Yes or No

My library at home had online databases containing newspaper and journal articles. Yes or No

My library at home provided space to work, study, and talk in groups. Yes or No

My library at home had wireless internet access for my laptop. Yes or No

My library at home offered classes on how to use the library. Yes or No

My library at home was a comfortable place to study. Yes or No

My library at home let me bring food and beverages into the building. Yes or No

My library at home had librarians who could help me with my research. Yes or No

My library at home collected monetary fines for overdue items. Yes or No

2. What did you like the most about your previous library?

3. Write a question you have about Galvin Library here.

Appendix D: Library Checklist for New Students

Your First Month at IIT: A Library Checklist

Week before classes:

☐ Walk around the Galvin Library to find where everything is. http://library.iit.edu/maps

☐ Read the Quick Tips & Tutorials. http://library.iit.edu/guides

First week of classes:

☐ Undergraduates: Find the call number of each of your textbooks. http://library.iit.edu/reserves

Graduates: There are very few graduate textbooks in the library. You should purchase your textbooks.

Location: Galvin Reserves (Library Use Only
Call Number: QD33.2.S552003
Text me this call number
Status: Available

Save the call number in your phone to save time at the Circulation Desk.

Second week of classes:

☐ Create your I-Share/IIT Account

⇒ http://library.iit.edu/ "My Library" on the right side.

⇒ Your "library borrower ID" is your IIT ID number that starts with an A. (A20..)

My Library

My I-Share/IIT Account   ᵃame:
MyILL Account
Course Reserves: vord:
E-Reserves & Textbooks
                    s a   Yes (Check "Ye
                    private   catalog will log you
                    workstation?

                    Login

2 ⟶ Create New Account

Third week of classes:

☐ Read your major's Research Guide

⇒ Learn which databases have articles on your subject and get search tips.

⇒ http://library.iit.edu/subjects

Materials Engineering Tags: metallurgy metallurgical_engine
Resources for research in the materials engineering discipline
Last update: Jun 10th, 2010 | URL: http://guides.library.iit.edu/materia

Home | Books | Articles and Databases | Websites

Add these tasks and the Library Events calendar to your Google Calendars.

Search for galvininstruction@gmail.com inside Google Calendar.

Chapter 3

Creating Research Ambassadors: Expanding the Role of International Students

Elys Kettling Law and Nicola Kille

This chapter describes a collaborative initiative undertaken by the College of Wooster Libraries and the College's student Ambassadors Program to gain insight into the experiences of and perceptions held by currently enrolled, undergraduate international students that may influence their library research behaviors, and to create avenues for these students to have greater agency in the design and delivery of enhanced library services for them. The "Research Ambassador" Initiative built upon the Ambassadors Program requirements for home country research, reflective documentation, and presentations to various audiences; and incorporated a series of activities to discover Ambassador research understandings and library use patterns, from high school through college. Through the Initiative, student Ambassadors from Africa, the Caribbean, Europe, and South Asia revealed strong associations with libraries as facilities and repositories of research resources, but little connection with librarians or library staff as part of their research referral and support network. Ambassador presentations to College of Wooster Libraries employees enhanced country cultural understandings about libraries and research, and helped identify possible ways to overcome real or perceived barriers to international student research in the College of Wooster Libraries.

Introduction

It has been anecdotally reported at both small colleges and large universities in the U. S. Midwest that international undergraduate students generally underutilize the academic library and its research support services. This is consistent with our experience at the College of Wooster. Although a significant portion of our student population is international, we rarely see these students looking for materials in the stacks, using either phone, online or in-person reference services, or taking advantage of opportunities for research consultations with subject specialist librarians. Where we do see them congregating is at the Libraries' circulation desks.

The College Libraries are one of the largest campus employers of international students. Their employment has predominantly been in library circulation services, an area where knowledge of English language subtleties is typically not required, nor is there any expectation for research referral. We have discovered however, that the library circulation desks, staffed during all open hours by international students, have indeed become a source of information referral. They are regularly used as access points by our international student community for information of all kinds, from the hottest social events on campus, to the best sources and strategies for a research assignment. Although this could possibly be attributed to the comfort associated with familiar language, trusted friends, and cultural norms of help seeking behavior, we are concerned with potential constraints posed by such limited consultation for research inquiry.

The Institution

The College of Wooster is a nationally recognized, private, four-year liberal arts college, located in Wooster, Ohio. It has an enrollment of approximately 2000 students, and confers the degrees of Bachelor of Arts, Bachelor of Music, and Bachelor of Music Education. For more than sixty years, a hallmark of the College of Wooster experience has been the completion by each graduating senior of a year long, Independent Study (IS) in which the student works one-on-one with a faculty mentor to conceive, organize, and complete a significant work of inquiry or creative expression on a topic of his or her own choosing.

The College Mission

The College of Wooster is a community of independent minds, working together to prepare students to become leaders of character and influence in an interdependent global community. We engage motivated students in a rigorous and dynamic liberal education. Mentored by a faculty nationally recognized for excellence in teaching, Wooster graduates are creative and independent thinkers with exceptional abilities to ask important questions, research complex issues, solve problems, and communicate new knowledge and insight (College of Wooster, 2010, inside front cover).

International Student Population

In Fall 2010, international students comprised just over seven percent of the enrolled student population at the College, and represented more than thirty countries. They include students with citizenship outside the United States, exchange students, and global nomads. As a requirement for admission, they must have demonstrated competency in English, most often by a Test of English as a Foreign Language (TOEFL) minimum score of 550 out of a possible 677 (paper based) or 80 out of a possible 120 (Internet based), or an International English Language Testing System (IELTS) minimum band of 7.0 out of a possible 9.0 (College of Wooster, 2010, 250–251).

The Initiative

This initiative began with a conversation around a lunch table. Elys, the College's Reference and Instruction Librarian, mentioned her concern that College of Wooster international students were not taking full advantage of available undergraduate research support services, particularly reference assistance and research consultations with subject area librarians. She shared her desire to investigate the factors behind this, noting a difficulty finding insights in the academic library literature directly applicable to undergraduate international students from a wide cross section of world regions, with no need for ESL classes, and enrolled in small, research intensive, liberal arts colleges. A person across the table piped up, "You know, my students might be able to help you out with that. We should talk." It was Nicola, Coordinator of the College of Wooster Ambassadors Program.

The College of Wooster Ambassadors Program

The College of Wooster has had a formal Ambassadors Program since 2001. The program is designed, in general, to foster "an understanding of the local, situated in a broader context" and more specifically, to "[bring] the world to Wooster, [allowing] the voices of diverse international and global nomad students to be heard on our campus, and beyond" (College of Wooster Ambassadors Program, 2011).

In the program, five College of Wooster international students or global nomads claiming different "home" countries are selected each spring, from a competitive application process, to serve as Ambassadors for the following year. To be selected as Ambassadors, students must either be natives of, or have lived for several years in, a country other than the United States.

A year of Ambassador service begins with a summer research fellowship in which students execute a personal "research agenda" that guides their gathering of information and cultural artifacts from their home country that they will use in teaching others about their nation and culture. In their summer research, Ambassadors are encouraged to use a broad range of information sources, and cautioned against over reliance on the Internet. When the Ambassadors return to the College the subsequent fall, they draw upon their personal experiences, along with their summer research information, to provide interactive presentations on their country to local school groups and community organizations, inform discussions in college courses, and plan intercultural community events.

Through these activities, the Ambassadors Program seeks to develop Ambassador leadership skills, research skills, presentation skills, enhanced self-confidence, and opportunities for creative expression. For the Wooster community, it hopes to extend country understandings beyond typical textbook treatments, correct misconceptions about individual countries and regions, remove some of the "exoticism" associated with Ambassadors' homes and lives, and to provide forums for questions to be asked and answered by engaging individuals with direct, long-standing, and contemporary experience in international settings (College of Wooster Ambassadors Program, 2011).

Creating "Research Ambassadors"

That initial conversation between Elys and Nicola was timed fortuitously: the 2010–2011 Ambassadors had been selected, and they were working on their summer research agendas. The conversation prompted consideration of the College Libraries as a new Ambassadors Program audience. In the Ambassadors, Elys could find not only authentic voices for College of Wooster international student experiences with research, but also individuals eager to share those experiences with an inquisitive Wooster community. In the Libraries, the Ambassadors could find not only a new and inquisitive audience who were enthusiastic to learn from the students, but also one eager to help them with their research.

Nicola and Elys realized their programs shared research skill development as a common objective, and an emphasis on primary sources as a common value, and they were both excited by the prospect of a more collaborative and integrative relationship between the Ambassadors and the Libraries.

Together, they developed an initiative to expand the existing student Ambassador role to include that of international student "Research Ambassador." Under this initiative, Ambassadors would have several venues to reflect upon and share, with each other and with library employees, the research experiences they had had in high school and college; could interpret, comment upon, and question library practices in both settings; could corroborate or refute cultural assumptions; and could provide library employees with context for interpreting and responding to observed patterns in international student research behavior.

Research Ambassador Initiative Activities

Upon their return from their summer, home country research, Research Ambassadors were asked to:

1. Reflect upon and document the research activities they engaged in while at home, including any contact made with libraries.
2. Compare their summer research process to the kind of research activities they have engaged in thus far in the context of their College of Wooster academic program.

3. Participate in a focus group, led by the Reference and Instruction Librarian, discussing their experiences, observations, and associations with libraries and research, from high school through college, and providing opportunities to identify those aspects most and least helpful to them.

4. Provide evaluative commentary on their home country's treatment in a chapter from a contemporary reference work typically used to provide guidance for culturally sensitive interactions with persons from specific international countries.

5. Prepare a presentation for College of Wooster Libraries employees to enhance specific country cultural understandings about libraries and research, and identify possible ways to overcome real or perceived barriers to international student research in the College of Wooster Libraries.

Fall 2010 Pilot of the Research Ambassador Initiative

General Demographics of the Pilot Group

The five "Research Ambassadors" in the pilot initiative claimed home countries in Africa, the Caribbean, Europe, and South Asia. There were three females and two males. Three students had attended public high schools in their home countries, and two had attended private high schools there. In Fall 2010, one student was a sophomore, three were juniors, and one was a College of Wooster senior. Four of the five had attended the College as first year students, and one transferred in as a sophomore. The Ambassadors' intended majors were Political Science/Economics (double major), Mathematics/Physics (double major), Geology major/Mathematics minor, Economics, and Neuroscience.

Caveats Regarding Ambassador Participation in Initiative Activities

The 2010–2011 Ambassadors were told about the Research Ambassador (RA) Initiative before embarking on their summer research fellowships. They were given an outline of the five activities involved, and told the overall purpose was to learn more about the research habits and expectations of undergraduate international students at the College, in order to discover possible ways to enhance the College Libraries' support of that research. Although the Ambassadors were well suited to help answer questions about international students and their research, they were assured, as with all other presentation and question answering opportunities in the Ambassadors Program, they would not be expected, and certainly not required, to answer any question or discuss any subject about which they were uncomfortable. They were also assured written documents completed for the initiative had no specified length or expected academic format to which they needed to adhere. The only stated expectations were that communication be thoughtful, honest, and as clear/complete as reasonably possible.

Timing of Initiative Activities

To ensure the Ambassadors had opportunities to address each of the five Research Ambassador Initiative activities before the close of the Fall 2010 semester, and to anticipate typical surges in academic semester and Ambassadorial responsibilities, specific due dates were attached to each of the five RA activities. Although the students completed all five Research Ambassador activities during the fall semester, getting them to submit their initial responses regarding their summer research was difficult, until Elys and Nicola learned the reason for the delay. In one of their weekly Ambassador meetings, Ambassadors shared their concern that they document the "right" summer research activities in the "right" way. This revelation was surprising, because in past years, Ambassadors had documented their summer research activities without any difficulty: it is a standard requirement of the Ambassadors Program. Apparently, the idea of sharing that kind of documentation with a group outside the Ambassadors Program, e.g. the Libraries, created a perception of heightened expectations and more critical evaluation, particularly in the context of calling it "research."

To allay these concerns, parallel and consistent assurances were provided: there were *no wrong answers* to any of the RA questions, including those about the Ambassadors' summer research, except that they "did not do any research over the summer." The latter would only be "wrong" because summer research is required in the Ambassadors Program. Furthermore, to move the Ambassadors away from reliance on a right/wrong dichotomy, it was suggested that the "best/most helpful" responses would be those indicating specifically whom or what was consulted as resources, the frequency of consultation, and why a particular research path was chosen. The combination of these communications opened the floodgates, and the responses were almost immediately forthcoming, continuing faithfully through to the end of the semester.

Activity 1: Reflect upon and document the research activities they engaged in while completing their summer home country research agenda, including any contact made with libraries.

The Ambassadors had quite varied summer research agendas, encompassing emphases on home country daily life, contemporary issues/events, historic perspectives, cultural traditions and norms, and integration of multicultural ethnic identities. Their stated agendas were:

- Daily life in my country in response to questions people have asked me repeatedly since I have been in the United States
- Perspectives across my home country on contemporary events/issues affecting persons living there
- The broad history of my country and my hometown over the past eighty years
- The culture, traditions, superstitions, and ethnic norms in my home country from a viewpoint of greater awareness/consciousness [In the Ambassadors Program, this is often referred to as "acting as a tourist in your home country."]
- Integration of a cultural identity from one world region into my identity as a resident of a different culture/world region

Despite the diversity of research agendas, all five Ambassadors used interviewing as their primary summer research method, either face-to face, or online via Skype, and all five interviewed at least some persons they knew, either family, friends, relatives, or past acquaintances. All documented an intentional desire to get a broad range of perspectives, and to avoid the tendency to over-generalize; however, they undertook different means to gain those perspectives. Three of the five students reported interviewing three generations of persons for differing vantage points. One student did extensive cross-country travel, observing and conducting interviews at several stops along the way. One ensured she spoke directly with at least one person from each class and income group. Another reported such an extensive social network in his country that it was "safe to say most people our age are probably only separated by two degrees." This, combined with the network of his friends' relatives and acquaintances, gave him "way more options than [he] needed."

Three of the five Ambassadors kept abreast of home country news and local opinions via their local newspapers, television, radio, and on-line news outlets, making comparisons between those and coverage in international newspapers. The Internet was everyone's source for quick facts and statistics, although one Ambassador also personally contacted his country's National Statistical Office for data. He was disappointed the Office did not have any up-to-date information, and was told that "new information would be posted on their website 'soon'."

Only the European Ambassador reported using a library for any aspect of her summer research: she visited the local history section of her hometown public library to gather information. Otherwise, she noted, public libraries in her country are used primarily for "recreational purposes," and university libraries "tend not to be used much anymore" because "the Internet and other sources allow access to the same sources." The South Asian Ambassadors also noted a recreational reading focus in their public libraries, as well as the tendency for those facilities to have older print resources. The Caribbean Ambassador shared that he had never used his community library because of an involved and lengthy process to get a library card, including presentation of a tax registration number, and the African Ambassador said the use of a library was "not necessary," as his topic did not require he "consult books written by 'experts'."

Activity 2: Compare their summer research process to the kind of research activities they have engaged in thus far in the context of their College of Wooster academic program.

All five Ambassadors noted differences in their approach to their summer research from academic research they had been expected to do at the College. All mentioned the need to be prepared for a wide range of Ambassadors Program audiences, to anticipate their questions, and to find points of connection with them. The European Ambassador was looking for a "collection of stories and information" which she could "select and [draw] from to teach others about [her] country." The African Ambassador was looking for similarities and differences in values and preferences. A South Asian Ambassador was looking for local tie-ins to material presented in common college readings. The consensus seemed to be that the Ambassador research had more openness and subjectivity, whereas their experience with academic research to date was more objective and analytical. Three of their comparisons:

> Ambassador research is very different from the other research I have conducted. It's not as objective as putting two different chemicals in a test tube. Research for being an Ambassador is more like answering questions and looking at those topics in more depth and detail. (South Asian student)

> Research I have previously undertaken has been purely academic.... It often included the analysis of theories combined with an analysis of certain data. Also, it was always clearly set up in a formal research design, including hypotheses and operationalization of variables. For the Ambassadors Program, the research was quite different. Instead of doing focused, narrow, and specific research, I set out to gather a broad knowledge about my country. However, my previous experience with data and research did help me navigate through the many different sources available and also to gather specific numbers and data. (European student)

For the research I did at home, the answers involved more time collecting and compiling the data, whereas research as a college student not only requires one to collect and compile data, but to really look into the conclusions drawn and analyze them. (Caribbean student)

The Caribbean Ambassador further elaborated on differences in his understanding of research expectations by academic discipline:

Having taken mostly science and math classes, I haven't done many research papers, but rather analytical or lab report type papers. These papers tend to involve solving a problem, based on topics learned in class and meeting with professors [to] get a specific solution, rather than papers in the arts and social sciences where there is a wealth of varying opinions and many more options (usually requiring a literature review).

Activity 3: Participate in a focus group, led by the Reference and Instruction Librarian, discussing their experiences, observations, and associations with libraries and research, from high school through college, and providing opportunities to identify those aspects most and least helpful to them.
The focus group was scheduled for an hour during what normally would be an Ambassadors Program weekly meeting time. All five Ambassadors participated, and the conversation was, in a word, "lively." This was the first activity of the Research Ambassador Initiative where the Ambassadors were together as a group. Below are the question tracks receiving the most extensive discussion.

Describe the kinds of research assignments you had in high school.
Two Ambassadors reported not having to do any research assignments in high school. Both indicated the emphasis in their high school was on examination preparation. The other three Ambassadors reported doing research papers ranging in length from five to twenty pages and in

sources from five to "as many as possible." The student reporting having completed a twenty-page paper in high school noted all her papers were handwritten, which translates to five to seven typewritten pages. Paper topics were general in nature, e.g. on a particular population, global issue, or scientific phenomenon.

Where did you get your information for these high school research assignments?

Two of the three Ambassadors who had completed high school research assignments listed identical sources: online encyclopedias, the Internet, and subject specific textbooks. The third Ambassador, a student who had attended an International Baccalaureate academy, was the only one to mention the use of online, full text article databases in her high school research, specifically "JSTOR and Ebsco."

Describe your use of libraries in your home country through high school.

Public library use was mentioned by four of the Ambassadors, primarily as a place to find newspapers, magazines, and pleasure reading/fiction. All five students had a high school library, and spent at least some portion of their school day in it. One Ambassador reported going there to read the newspaper, but the other four noted the high school library was where you went if you wanted to skip class, had detention, or needed to hide.

When you think of a library, what four words/phrases come to mind?

Their word sets:
- Articles, books, computers, quiet
- Books, research, authors, shhhh
- Reservoir of knowledge resources
- A source of information
- Information, access, studying, resources

When you think of the College of Wooster Libraries, what four words/phrases come to mind?

Their word sets:

- Carrel, MacLab, Study Rooms, I.S. [Independent Study]
- Printing, Writing Center, IT [Information Technology], Study Room
- Homework, Printing, Hang out, Check emails
- Paper transformed into a clear, organized, work of art
- Information, access, studying, resources

Conspicuously absent from either set of library word associations are any mentions of *people.*

How often do you use one or more of the College of Wooster Libraries?

Four of the five Ambassadors indicated using one or more of the College of Wooster Libraries "at least once per day." The fifth Ambassador reported using it "at least once per month."

If you've ever used the College of Wooster Libraries or its resources, for which of the following activities did you use it?

Table 3.1: Reported Use of the College Libraries by Research Ambassadors	
Place to study Place to find a book Place to order a book from another library	5 Ambassadors
Place to meet friends Place to access a full text article database Place to order an article from another library Place to get items on Reserve	4 Ambassadors
Place of their student employment	3 Ambassadors (Two Ambassadors work for the Libraries. The third works for Campus Security and conducts Security rounds in the Libraries.)

(Table 3.1 continued)

Table 3.1: Reported Use of the College Libraries by Research Ambassadors	
Place to find a magazine, journal, or newspaper Place to watch a film Place to check out a film Place to eat/have a beverage	2 Ambassadors
Place to attend a library instruction class Place to consult with a research librarian Place to lounge/nap	1 Ambassador
Place to check out language CD/tape	No Ambassadors

When you have a research assignment, who are the persons you consult to guide you or help you complete the assignment?

All five Ambassadors would consult their course professors; three would consult their peers/classmates, if permissible; one would consult the College's Writing Center (housed in the Libraries); one would consult their Teaching Apprentice (upper level undergraduate student helping the course professor); and one would try to find guidance from the literature. None mentioned they would consult a librarian or any member of the library staff. Their individual responses follow.

I would consult
- Professors, authors of articles, books
- Professors, Teaching Apprentices, peers
- The teacher, maybe classmates if allowed
- My professor and maybe my classmates
- Professor for that course and the Writing Center

Do you know any students who work in the College of Wooster Libraries?

The answer to this was a resounding, "Yes!" with numbers ranging from ten to more than thirty students. Three of the five Ambassadors knew more than thirty students.

Besides Elys, do you know any staff members or faculty who work in the College of Wooster Libraries?

One Ambassador reported knowing no one except Elys. One reported knowing a few persons by face, but had "no personal connections" with any library employee. The three students employed in the Libraries knew three to five library staff members, most often their immediate supervisors.

What do you like most about the College of Wooster Libraries?

Three Ambassadors mentioned the availability of group study rooms, one mentioned the "wide selection of resources," and one mentioned the Macintosh computer lab. Two expressed feeling quite comfortable in the College Libraries, akin to "living there;" one for the computer access, since her own computer had crashed, and the other for spaces to relax, eat, and socialize.

What do you like least about the College of Wooster Libraries?

For this question, each Ambassador mentioned something different. One mentioned her inability to study in the Libraries because of distractions from her large circle of friends checking in. Another mentioned that the group study rooms fill up quickly and other spaces can be too noisy. A third mentioned the datedness and slowness of the public computers. A fourth mentioned the marked difference in the quality of the study carrels between the Timken Science Library and the Andrews/Gault Main library. The fifth Ambassador indicated he could not think of anything to dislike.

What is most confusing about the College of Wooster Libraries?

Three Ambassadors found the Libraries' website confusing. One found knowing what was on each of the five floors of the Main library confusing. Another found the Andrews/Gault Library distinction within the Main library confusing, especially because both Andrews and Gault libraries flow from one into the other across several floors of a single, very large building.

Activity 4: Provide evaluative commentary on their home country's treatment in a chapter from a contemporary reference work typically used to provide guidance for culturally sensitive interactions with persons from specific international countries.

For this activity, specific country segments from one of two works were distributed for the Ambassadors to review, either the 2009 *Culturegrams: World Edition* or the 2006 edition of Morrison and Conaway's, *Kiss, Bow, or Shake Hands: The Bestselling Guide to Doing Business in More than 60 Countries.* The Morrison and Conaway book did not have a chapter for every single Ambassador home country; therefore, when Morrison and Conaway did not supply a relevant chapter, the appropriate *Culturegrams* country document was used instead.

The Ambassadors had little difficulty with this activity, and provided extensive commentary on the texts' treatment of the respective countries. In general, it was noted that historical backgrounds on their countries were fairly accurate, but that the works were missing key events and biographical details from the last seven to ten years. Uniformly, surprise was expressed at the generalizations offered regarding social norms, gender roles, and youth culture, many of which they perceived as having shifted in the last five years, if they ever were true in the past. Several Ambassadors asked about Morrison and Conaway's research methodology, wondering if they had personally visited the countries, had ever lived there, and if so, for how long. They questioned whether native residents were contacted for input, and if all age, social, and economic groups were represented in any inquiries made. Also, given the datedness of the some of the information, they wondered how recently there had been author contact with their country. Essentially, the Ambassadors held the reference work authors to the same standards of authenticity and representativeness they had set for themselves in conducting their summer home country research.

Activity 5: Prepare a presentation for College of Wooster Libraries employees to enhance specific country cultural understandings about libraries and research, and to identify possible ways to over-

come real or perceived barriers to international student research in the College of Wooster Libraries.

At the end of the Fall 2010 semester, the Ambassadors provided presentations to about half of the College Libraries' employees. Each student presented for seven to ten minutes, and then opened the floor for questions. They took the perspective of first year students from their home countries, noting differences between what would probably be a typical student's high school experience, and what they would discover at The College of Wooster.

An African Ambassador shared that in his country, the expected role of teachers is to pass on their knowledge to students. In his high school, there were no expectations for research papers, and he had no access to computers at home. Power outages were frequent. The school library provided all the textbooks needed for classes. He was disappointed to discover the College Libraries did not have any of his course textbooks, and that he was expected to buy them. However, he was pleasantly surprised to find the Libraries had quiet group study rooms where he could study without interruptions. He was not expecting the research required in his First Year Seminar (FYS), and it was his FYS professor who made him an appointment with a librarian to help him learn how to use college library resources and databases.

The South Asian Ambassadors shared a home country expectation that "substantial" and "authoritative" information would be provided to them by "professors." They were both overwhelmed by the sheer volume of books in the College Libraries from which to choose and the First Year Seminar requirement that they cite all their sources. Particularly challenging for them were their professors' requirements for in-text citation. One of these Ambassadors enlisted the aid of the Writing Center to help with these citations, and the other reviewed several classmates' papers to understand the required format. Both South Asian Ambassadors indicated being surprised at discovering a Media Library within the College Libraries.

A European Ambassador shared that she was very comfortable using her high school library. It was staffed not by librarians, but by mothers of the students. This Ambassador wrote several research papers in high school, and when she needed inspiration or information for a paper, she would simply browse the relevant library book section. She initially found the College of Wooster Libraries' arrangement of materials very confusing, as it "used letters instead of numbers," and reported having great difficulty finding books in the location indicated by the floor directory: every time she went to the floor listed for a call letter range, items with those letters were nowhere to be found. It took her several weeks before she realized this was due to a difference in the way floors are numbered in the United States. In her home country, the ground floor is the "zero" floor, and the floor above that is the "first" floor. In the College of Wooster Libraries, the "first" floor is the ground floor, and the floor above it is the "second" floor. Small nuances such as these can make a difference to a new student from another country or culture.

A Caribbean Ambassador reported avoiding his high school library as much as possible. He described it as "smaller than this classroom" [where the presentation was being held], with two small sections: fiction and textbooks "from the 1980s." His high school library was monitored by school prefects and managed by a librarian who would rap students' hands with a ruler if they were caught "disrespecting" the materials (e.g. creasing a text spine, dog-earring a page) or breaking the "quiet rule." He informed the group he has not needed to use the College of Wooster Libraries for research much yet, preferring to start with online sources and the readings recommended by his professor, then locating a few library books as necessary to "fill in the gaps."

Conclusions and Future Directions

The College of Wooster Research Ambassador Initiative was developed in response to gaps: an observed gap in library research support utilization by the College's international students, a gap in the Libraries' understanding of reasons behind this observation, and a gap in the library literature having direct application to the academic library relationship with international undergraduate students in small, private, liberal arts colleges. The Research Ambassador (RA) Initiative was the beginning of an effort to bridge some of these gaps through a series of conversations between the College Libraries and a small, but enthusiastic, subset of the College's international student population, the students in the College's Ambassadors Program.

Through the RA Initiative, the Libraries hoped to discover possible reasons for international students' lack of connection with library reference and research support services, and ways to facilitate those connections. We considered as explanations possible dissatisfaction with available resources, confusing communications, discomfort in the facilities, or experiences with cultural insensitivity; however, based on the information shared by the Research Ambassadors, none of those rationales directly applied. Whether claiming home countries in Africa, the Caribbean, Europe, or South Asia, Ambassadors reported being both quite comfortable in and satisfied with the College Libraries, regularly frequenting them to access computers, print and make copies, study, relax, check in with friends, check out materials, or to staff a shift at a circulation desk. While this group would appreciate clearer library floor signage, better/faster public computers, and library availability of course textbooks, lack of these things is treated as an inconvenience, not a significant deterrent to library use. The Research Ambassador Initiative taught us to investigate more closely these students' experiences in their high schools and highlighted some recurring themes. We refer to these themes as the *Three Rs—Research, Relationships,* and *Referral.*

From the beginning of the Research Ambassador Initiative, Ambassadors struggled with various contextual meanings for *research.* In their high schools, original research was not expected. Writing a research paper, if it was even required, meant compiling facts gleaned from teachers and textbooks, then fleshing these out with details from general online encyclopedias and statistical sources, usually without citation. At the College of Wooster, depending on the course and the discipline, research could mean exploring a focused topic through the scholarly literature, conducting experiments using the scientific method, engaging primary sources through ethnographic studies, developing predictive mathematical models, or creating a symphony. Success in these kinds of complex research endeavors requires the ability to ground inquiry in the work of preceding scholars and to conduct sophisticated searches of academic literature, databases, and data sets, within and across disciplines. These are not intuitive skills for any undergraduate student, and development of them requires collaborative efforts on the part of the teaching faculty and subject area librarians to create opportunities for students to learn, practice, and apply them at several points throughout their course of study. Through the Initiative, we discovered a tendency for Ambassadors to seek out research assistance from only half of that collaborative equation, their course professors.

The Ambassadors shared a common starting point for their research: consultation of persons with whom they had established *relationships*. For their home country research interviews, they began by contacting relatives, friends, and past acquaintances, then branched out from there, to persons they did not know, but whose perspective or expertise fit the research agenda. The Ambassadors reported using similar processes to gain information for their various College research projects, consulting first their professors for advice, then their classmates, then their circles of friends. Once help from these relationships has been exhausted, they would venture out to find research information on their own, most often by browsing the library book stacks and reviewing full text article databases. None mentioned seeking help from a librarian.

In general, this Ambassadors group reported negative associations with libraries and librarians in their home countries. Few had ever used a public library. Their high school libraries were often quite small facilities, providing access to course textbooks, a limited range of curriculum specific, print materials, and in some cases, a small set of online databases. The library atmosphere reflected hushed silence, and library staff maintained strict discipline, even to the point of physical punishment for rule infractions. If a student was sent to the library, it was usually for detention, and if they went in of their own accord, it was often to hide. The safest approach was to avoid contact with or notice by any members of the library staff. Therefore, it is not surprising that in the College Libraries, these students' first inclination is to avoid initiating conversation or consultation with librarians, especially those not known by the students in any other relational context.

For this Ambassador group, an important key to building their relational networks for research appears to be *referral* from trusted persons with whom they have strong, existing connections. In their high school settings, the trusted source for "authoritative" and "substantial" information was the teacher. In the college setting, that role has shifted to their course professors. Although College of Wooster professors regularly refer their students to the Libraries for research information, in the case of international students lacking a positive history with librarians, this type of referral has the potential to be interpreted simply as a suggestion to visit the library facilities or website to check for research sources. If these students have difficulty independently locating material in the stacks, or effectively navigating the array of online library databases, they can easily conclude research in their area of inquiry is not available. For this student population, it would be helpful for professors to either make individual student referrals to specific librarians by name, with appropriate topic and personal introductions, or to collaboratively work with librarians to engage international students in library instruction sessions where they have significant opportunities to positively interact with both their professor and a librarian in the context of their research.

Professors, however, are not the only trusted referral sources for international students: their international student peers are as well. Each Research Ambassador knows at least ten other international students working in the College Libraries, and most know more than thirty students employed there. The Research Ambassadors Initiative grew out of a concern about research source referrals coming from this large network of international student friends staffing shifts at College Libraries' circulation desks, without the benefit of any specialized research training. Two of the Research Ambassadors are library circulation desk employees who before the Initiative did not know any librarians. Through the conversations around and during the Research Ambassador Initiative, they have become more familiar with Elys and her interest in supporting international student research. These students are now in a much better position to make referrals to her, as a librarian with whom they have developed a semester long relationship, and whom they understand wants to lift up and learn from the voices of international students, instead of shushing them quiet.

Future Directions

The Research Ambassador Initiative marks the beginning of a collaborative conversation between the College of Wooster Libraries and the College Ambassadors Program that we believe, extended across several Ambassador cohorts, has the potential to enhance our understanding of the research expectations, needs, and preferences of our international student community, and to give that community a means of regular and direct communication with the College Libraries. The conversations are far from complete. For the Research Ambassadors from Africa, the Caribbean, Europe and South Asia, the themes of research, relationships, and referral were consistent and prominent. We need to determine if these same themes are salient for students from other world regions such as South America, East Asia, or the Middle East, or for other sets of students from the same regions as the pilot RA group. We also need to determine how representative Ambassadors are of the diversity within the College of Wooster international student community. Individuals chosen to be international student Ambassadors tend to be some of the College's most outgoing, confident, active, and academically gifted students.

Our plans are to continue the Research Ambassador Initiative for at least two more years, to see whether or not currently observed behavioral and conversational patterns hold true for subsequent Ambassadors, and what impact the RA Initiative might have on international students' use and promotion of research support systems in the College Libraries. Given the extended relational network reported by Research Ambassadors, the Initiative has the potential to reach a significant portion of the international student community in a relatively short time. In Spring 2011, the pilot Research Ambassadors will introduce the RA Initiative to the 2011–2012 Ambassadors and to Elys, their Ambassadors Program librarian. The 2011–2012 Ambassadors will also be introduced to the subject librarians in their intended majors, and given an opportunity in Spring 2012 to collaboratively create a multimedia guide to the College Libraries' staff and services for use in new international student orientation. Our hope is to pave the way for referrals and relationship building with the next Research Ambassadors group in a manner consistent with the values and preferences shared by the pilot group, and to show successive Research Ambassador cohorts the interconnectedness of their roles in developing a more responsive and supportive campus environment for international student research.

The Research Ambassadors Initiative would not have been possible or as promising without the support and dedication of the five Research Ambassadors who bravely engaged in those early conversations with us. We are especially grateful to these students who challenged us, throughout the pilot Initiative, to find common relational ground before asking difficult questions, and to remain in conversation long enough to discover authentic, substantial answers.

References

College of Wooster. 2010. *Catalogue: 2010–2011*. Wooster, OH: The College of Wooster.

College of Wooster Ambassadors Program. 2011. "About the Program." Accessed January 24. http://www.wooster.edu/Offices-Directories/Center-for-Diversity-and-Global-Engagement/Ambassadors-Program/About-the-Program.

CultureGrams. 2009. World ed. Ann Arbor, MI: Proquest.

Morrison, Terri and Wayne A. Conaway. 2006. *Kiss, Bow, or Shake Hands: The Bestselling Guide to Doing Business in More the 60 Countries*. 2nd ed. Avon, MA: Adams Media.

Further Reading

DiMartino, Diane and Lucinda R. Zoe. 2000. "International Students and the Library: New Tools, New Users, and New Instruction." In *Teaching the New Library to Today's Users,* edited by Trudi E. Jacobson and Helene C. Williams, 17–43. New York: Neal-Schuman.

Knight, Lorrie, Maryann Hight, and Lisa Polfer. 2010. "Rethinking the Library for the International Student Community." *Reference Services Review* 38 (4): 581–605.

Montgomery, Catherine. 2010. *Understanding the International Student Experience.* New York: Palgrave Macmillan.

Chapter 4

Engaging International Students in Academic Library Initiatives for their Peers

Dawn Amsberry and Loanne Snavely

Through a student internship program, the Penn State University Librar-ies further extended their programming efforts for international students to include engaging student peers in building collections and services for international students. The internships are designed to give stu-dents professional experience in their fields through library initiatives. This project focused on the largest international student population—those from China—and resulted in several peer-to-peer initiatives in-cluding a new collection of popular literature in Chinese, an audio tour in Chinese, and blog, Facebook and Twitter posts in both Chinese and English to market the initiatives.

Introduction

The University Libraries at Penn State have been providing a variety of special programming for international students to engage them with the library and the resources available to them for over thirty years. These have included orientations specifically for international students with an introduction to their disciplinary library and librarian subject specialist, an essay contest, training programs for staff on working with international students, library programs for visiting international scholars, focus groups with international students, and other initia-tives.

We have continued to explore ways to more fully reach out to the international academic community. A series of focus groups with international students provided excellent ideas for new initiatives. In addition, we garnered suggestions from the literature, such as Chau's (2002, 392) recommendation to provide multilingual library materials in an effort to create a welcoming atmosphere and promote good customer service. We began brainstorming a list of possible projects, programs and initiatives related to areas we identified based on our research and feedback from the focus groups.

We also began exploring strategies for implementation. The Bednar Internship, a program already established in the libraries through an endowment, was designed for undergraduate students to learn and gain practical experience in their profession through a library internship. A number of these internships are available each year, and library faculty can submit proposals for appropriate projects. This seemed an ideal way to combine our programming ideas with effective peer input and collaboration, resulting in our focus on reaching students with introductory material in their first language, providing leisure reading in their home language, and engaging student peers in building collections and services for international students as our top priorities.

The Institution

Penn State University, often described as "one university geographically dispersed," is a land-grant institution with twenty-four campuses around the state of Pennsylvania, including a medical school and a law school, as well as the World Campus, an online campus with over 8,000 students. In Fall 2010 Penn State's overall student population was nearly 100,000, including over 77,000 undergraduates and 10,000 graduate and professional students in addition to the World Campus. The University Park campus located in the center of the state hosts 38,000 undergraduates and 6,000 graduate students, making it the largest of the University's locations. Although Penn State is a large and disperse institution, most first-year students at University Park indicate a strong sense of belonging at the University within their first few weeks on campus, and most describe Penn State as a welcoming community (Penn State University 2010).

The Penn State University Libraries, with locations at all Penn State campuses, hold over five million volumes and are currently ranked seventh among the top ten research libraries in North America by the Association of Research Libraries. At the University Park campus, there are thirteen specialized subject libraries housed in six buildings, including one of the largest maps collections in the country and a renowned Special Collections Library. The department of Library Learning Services, the sponsor for the initiative described in this chapter, is located in the Pattee Library at University Park and oversees the Libraries' instructional activities, conducts outreach to international students and other constituencies, and provides general reference and referral services.

Cultural Context

Penn State's excellent academic programs, especially those in the earth sciences and engineering, have been drawing large numbers of international students for over a century. In Fall 2010, 5,000 international students were enrolled at Penn State, the highest enrollment ever. Slightly more than half were graduate students, indicating an increase in the percentage of undergraduates over previous years. The vast majority of international students (4,436 in 2010) make their home at the University Park campus, located in a beautiful rural valley in central Pennsylvania, surrounded by mountains and trees. Although this natural setting may be very different from their home environments, international students have found other ways to stay connected to their home communities, including sixty-eight international and multicultural student clubs and organizations. New international students may arrive without a place to live, and without knowing anyone in the community. Sometimes they are travelling for the first time in their lives, and may be in the United States for the first time. They are often excellent students, graduating at the tops of their classes, and very serious about their studies. For many of these reasons, international students tend to make firm associations with the library. They may live a distance from campus, study in the library frequently, and appreciate the services provided.

About twenty-seven percent of Penn State's international students come from China and Taiwan, making Chinese speakers the largest portion of our international student body. By contrast, the second and third largest country groups, India and Korea, constitute about sixteen percent and fifteen percent, respectively. Most of the Chinese and Taiwanese students are enrolled in graduate and professional programs (see table 1). Chinese students are active in many venues on campus, including the International Student Council, the Chinese Undergraduate Student Association, the Hong Kong Student Association, and the Traditional Chinese Tea Ceremony Club. In addition to the student population, Penn State also hosted 300 international scholars and faculty from China in 2009. Because the Chinese student population at Penn State is by far the largest international population, and because the next largest population (India) traditionally has a very firm foundation in the English language, we decided to focus this effort to engage international students in the library on the Chinese-speaking population.

TABLE 4.1: Programs of Top Five Penn State International Student Populations, Fall 2009				
	Graduate	Undergraduate	Medical	Law
China	718	459	0	10
India	538	160	0	1
Korea	286	376	0	5
Taiwan	140	65	2	1
Malaysia	13	140	1	0

The Initiative

Previous success elsewhere in the library with undergraduate student library interns led us to develop a proposal for a paid, semester-long three-credit internship specifically for a native-Chinese-speaking international student who would assist us in developing services for Chinese students. While Penn State University Libraries are fortunate to have a donor-sponsored internship program for junior and senior undergraduates, libraries without outside funding could still develop a credit-bearing internship that would provide students with a chance to share their cultural background while gaining work experience. Additional benefits to the student could include a letter of recommendation for future employment as well as a portfolio of web-based projects and other concrete initiatives used by the library.

Although much has been written in the library literature about internships for MLIS graduate students, there are very few published articles that discuss undergraduate library interns. Harwood (2008), a business librarian who developed a three-credit library internship for undergraduate business majors, also notes the lack of literature on comparable programs. Harwood wanted an intern with a business background who would bring "an invaluable student perspective" to library services, and decided that an upper division business student would be an ideal candidate. Although the first intern in Harwood's program had career aspirations to become a business librarian, she notes that recruiting for the profession was not necessarily part of her original intent in developing the internship. In our case, none of the internship candidates expressed an interest in librarianship as a career; however, they all noted the importance of the skills incorporated into the internship, such as writing, translating, marketing, and communication, to their own career goals. This, in fact, is exactly what our particular internship was intended to do.

The University Libraries Bednar Internship is privately funded and open only to full-time juniors and seniors exhibiting academic excellence. The internship must be related to the students' field of study or career areas, and must constitute a "learning experience." The internship developed for the project outlined here consisted of 130 hours of work during one semester, and earned three credits through the College of Liberal Arts internship program. The intern was also paid the hourly equivalent of library wage level three employees. The job description indicated that the intern would assist in the Libraries' outreach efforts to international students, and investigate ways to further internationalize the Libraries. Projects included translating and recording the Libraries' audio tour into Chinese; recommending popular titles in Chinese for the Libraries leisure collection; translating or developing other library materials for international students; and participating in developing international-related Libraries programs. Fluency in Chinese, ability to translate written documents from English, and knowledge of popular Asian literature were required qualifications for the applicants.

We advertised the internship through various Asian student associations on campus, as well as through the Office of Global programs (the office on campus that supports international and study abroad students), and received nineteen enthusiastic responses from students. The applicants all described their desire to share their own culture with other students, as well as their interest in internationalizing the Libraries. One student mentioned her own difficulty adjusting socially to a new culture as the impetus for her interest in helping others. Another student highlighted her bicultural identity, describing how she embraced both American culture and the culture of her native Taiwan. Many of the respondents held leadership positions in student organizations, and many of them had experience in both oral and written translation.

Choosing from among these highly motivated and qualified applicants was a difficult task. Because the terms of the internship stipulate that the student must be a junior or senior, the five lower classmen and five graduate students who applied were ineligible. From the remaining pool of applicants, we chose four candidates for interviews, which included a Skype interview with a student who had already gone home to Taiwan. We ultimately selected two Chinese-speaking students for the internship, a senior comparative literature major from Hong Kong, and a junior public relations major from Taiwan. The students were chosen for their language skills as well as their interest in and knowledge of popular Chinese literature and culture. One student completed the internship in Fall 2009, and the other in Spring 2010.

In informal focus groups with international students previously conducted by the Libraries, students indicated a strong interest in leisure reading titles in their own languages. Several students mentioned the idea of an "international section" of the library, where foreign language titles would be housed together. This interest in popular foreign language titles is also apparent in a survey by Yi (2007, 671), in which one international student respondent suggested that the library collect more books "that are well known and popular in the country of publication." The Penn State University Libraries does collect a small number of popular titles in other languages, and also has a new English language leisure collection of about 3,000 titles located in a separate reading room, but popular foreign language titles had not been a focus of either of these collections. In response to suggestions from the focus groups, and in consultation with the librarian in charge of the Leisure Reading Collections, a top priority for the interns was the expansion of the leisure reading collection to include popular titles in Chinese. This project was particularly exciting for the interns, because it allowed them to bring in their own unique perspectives, selecting titles that they remembered from home and that they knew their peer international students would enjoy.

Using the websites Chinese Books Online and YesAsia, the interns developed a list of thirty titles consisting mainly of romance and adventure by popular Chinese authors that would appeal to Chinese international students. The emphasis on fiction was based on the interns' own interests as well as on research in the library literature indicating that fiction is by far the most popular genre in academic library leisure reading collections (Sanders 2009, 181). Examples of titles from the list include the Princess Pearl series by Qiong Yao, a popular trilogy that was made into a television drama, as well as *The God of Love* and *The Red Thread* by Giddens Ko. The list also included a few non-fiction titles, such as *The Third New York,* a book of travel essays by Pan Guoling written from the perspective of a visitor from Hong Kong. The interns also developed a list of Chinese language fiction and short stories currently owned by the Libraries and held in the regular stacks that could be incorporated into a leisure reading display on Chinese literature.

The list of new titles was submitted to the Libraries acquisition team, who ordered the books from a supplier in Taiwan, Lexis Book Company, using leisure reading collection funds. The Taiwan vendor supplied most of the titles, but some of them were not available through that vendor and had to be ordered through another vendor in Hong Kong, the Beijing Chinese Book Trading Company. Because of the time involved in ordering books from overseas, the acquisition of the Chinese titles took far longer than we anticipated. We had originally planned to involve the interns in a marketing campaign to publicize the new Chinese books once they were available; however, the books were not received in the Libraries until after the internships had ended.

With the opening of a new reading room, the Libraries held a series of themed leisure reading exhibits. In conjunction with Chinese New Year in 2011, we mounted a display of Chinese literature including the Chinese titles selected by the interns as well as novels in English by Chinese authors or set in China, and non-fiction titles on Chinese history and culture. The display was promoted through the Chinese student groups, the leisure reading blog, Facebook and Twitter posts, and the Office of Global Programs. We plan to solicit suggestions for additional titles in other languages from international students and incorporate these titles into other exhibits. These displays help create a welcoming atmosphere for international students, and encourage them to use the library. Ross (1999, 790) has noted that readers select "comfort reading" such as old favorites when they are under stress; such behavior may be particularly true of international students looking for a piece of home in a new environment.

In addition to the leisure book list, the interns' second major project was the translation and recording of an audio podcast tour of the Libraries' main buildings at University Park. Using the script from the Libraries' existing audio tour in English, the interns translated the written script into Chinese. The second intern further refined the script, and then recorded the twenty-minute tour in Mandarin using equipment and technical assistance from the Media Commons, an audio/video recording studio managed by Penn State Information Technology Services and located in the library. The Chinese tour is available as an MP3 file on our website (Penn State University Libraries 2010). We advertise the tour at our library orientation for international students each semester, on our web page for library tours and on our page specifically for international students, and also at the orientation for new international visiting scholars, many of whom are Chinese speakers who have had limited exposure to English.

Since the second intern was with us during Chinese New Year, we asked her to write a post for the leisure reading blog about Chinese literature in honor of the holiday. Her post, Ten Things About Chinese Literature, discussed the Chinese writing system, poetry, the genre of martial arts fiction, and humor in Chinese literature. She advertised both the blog entry and the Chinese podcast tour through posts on Facebook and Twitter. The Chinese Facebook posts prompted some puzzled questions and one complaint from other students about why entries were appearing in Chinese, and one library staff member assumed the posts were a mistake. The intern then began to write the posts in both English and Chinese. These were good lessons for us in developing our marketing approaches as we begin to promote these resources that are new to both those within and outside the library.

In addition to the podcast tour and the blog entry, the interns also both worked on the translation of a welcome letter for international students. Both the English and Chinese versions of the letter are now distributed at our library orientation for international students, which typically attracts between one to two hundred students in the fall, and thirty to forty students in the spring. We plan to recruit additional students to translate the letter into other languages that are widely spoken on our campus, including Korean and Japanese. While our international students generally have a very high proficiency in English, reading the letter in their native language may help them feel more welcome in the library.

As with any new library initiative, working with the interns presented challenges as well as rewards. We have developed five tips for ensuring successful internships:

Tip #1: Allot project time for the supervising librarian. Although both of the interns were highly motivated and worked independently, it was still necessary for the supervising librarian to meet with them each week to provide guidance, monitor progress, and to maintain regular communication throughout the semester. Because the Bednar internships give academic credit, they are intended to be a learning experience as well as a hands-on work experience. Thus, the supervising librarian must design meaningful projects for the students rather than routine tasks. As with any project, flexibility is critical. Our original intent for the interns to spend a portion of their hours publicizing the new collection of Chinese books could not be implemented since the titles were not received during the course of the internships, so we had to move on to alternative projects from among those originally identified.

Tip #2: Arrange for a physical workspace. An additional challenge we faced was finding workspace for the interns, who worked approximately ten hours a week during the course of the semester. As in most libraries, free office space is rare and in high demand in our buildings. The interns needed a computer with Internet access in order to work on the book lists and translation projects, and some degree of privacy and quiet since the translation work required a good deal of focus and concentration. We were fortunately able to arrange for our intern to share an office with another part-time employee just two doors away from the supervising librarian.

Tip #3: Develop strategies to work with language considerations. Neither of the librarians involved in supervising the interns had any knowledge of Chinese, so it was impossible for us to evaluate the quality of the translation work, and we were unable to provide the interns with any assistance with the technicalities of translation. While the interns were chosen for their high level of fluency in both Chinese and English, they still found it difficult to translate some of the library specific terms used in the tour script, such as "circulation desk." In describing a similar translation project Chau (2002, 391) notes that concerns about the quality of translation arose not from the language capabilities of the translators, who were all native speakers, but from the difficulty of ensuring that the services themselves were accurately translated. Some degree of quality control was built into the project, since both interns worked on the translation and could check each other's work, a practice also recommended by Downing and Klein (2001, 501). Library tours in Mandarin available from other academic library websites also proved to be useful tools for translating unfamiliar terms, as was the ACRL Instruction Section's glossary of international library terminology (ACRL 2008). Both of the interns also used their own network of resources for proof reading and suggestions, and one of the interns' father was a diplomat with extensive translation experience, which gave us another level of assurance.

Tip #4: Welcome student input. An issue inherent in any translation is the question of the extent to which the translator inserts her own voice into the translation task. One of the interns commented that the script for the English tour, which was written by a librarian, was too formal for students. Her inclination was to choose more colloquial terms for the Chinese version. In developing their own multilingual library tour, Downing and Klein (2001, 501) encouraged student translators to "select the expression they would use if they were speaking to a friend." Because of these frequent issues regarding word choice and level of formality, one intern indicated that for her the translation of the tour script (consisting of about 3,300 words in the English version) became a work of art rather than a simple translation task. Since the second intern actually recorded the tour, she also felt inclined to adjust the wording to suit her own style of speaking. As she commented, "During the process of recording, I would usually realize that I had chosen to use a language that sounds too literary and not friendly enough, so I would make changes to wordings and expressions on the spot." Since our goal with the project was to engage international students in initiatives for their peers, we felt that a tour that reflected the personality and style of the student translators was appropriate.

Tip #5: Plan ahead for revisions and updates. Now that the tour is complete and available on our website, we face an additional question: how to keep the tour updated. Because of multiple construction projects in our library related to the creation of a Knowledge Commons, physical aspects of the library buildings have changed, rendering portions of both the English and Chinese versions of the tour out of date.

The intern who recorded the tour has since graduated and returned home, so is not available to create updates. This problem also presents an ideal solution for continuing to engage students, which would be to periodically recruit international student volunteers skilled in translation who could update and re-record the tour in Chinese as well as in other languages. Given the enthusiasm for sharing their cultural backgrounds we've encountered among international students, we believe this project would be successful.

Conclusion

The two internships resulted in a positive expansion of the library's collections and services for international students, and judging by the final reports submitted by the interns, also proved to be a valuable learning experience for the students. As one intern wrote, the experience was "a great opportunity to take what we learned in the classroom and apply it directly to the real world." Working with the interns allowed us to gain new insight by allowing us to see the library through the perspective of students who brought aspects of their own culture and language to bear on their outlook. Both student interns had feet in both their home and American cultures, giving them a unique way of looking at their college experience.

Inspired by our work with the interns, we plan to carry on the initiatives begun during the internships in a number of ways. Following is a summary of our future plans for continuing to expand our collections and services for international students:

- Publicize the new Chinese leisure books to the Chinese student community, and solicit suggestions for additional foreign-language leisure titles from international students
- Update the Chinese audio tour, and recruit additional student volunteers to create new tours in other languages
- Invite volunteers to translate a welcome letter for international students in multiple languages widely spoken on our campus, to be distributed at our international student orientation
- Create a series of displays in our leisure area featuring inter-

national themes, such as Chinese New Year, International Education Week, Hispanic Heritage Month, International Holidays and Festivals

- Hold an open house for international students during Spring break (when international students are often on campus) to publicize library services and solicit feedback and suggestions for improvements

We believe that engaging student peers in developing these initiatives will create a welcoming atmosphere in the library for international students, and help them through what may at first seem like a daunting journey: adjusting to a new educational system, a new culture, a new language. Research suggests that international students may use their university libraries more often than their American counterparts (Liao, Finn and Lu 2005, 12), perhaps in part because the library provides them with a much-needed home away from home. Anecdotal evidence from students supports this assumption, as suggested by the student who commented after one of our library orientation sessions, "I know I will visit here often."

References

ACRL Instruction Section. 2008. "Instruction for Diverse Populations Multilingual Glossary—Language Table." ACRL, http://www.ala.org/ala/mgrps/divs/acrl/about/sections/is/projpubs/languagetble.pdf.

Chau, May Ying. 2002. "Helping Hands: Serving and Engaging International Students." *The Reference Librarian* (79): 383–393.

Downing, Arthur and Leo Robert Klein. 2001. "A Multilingual Virtual Tour for International Students: The Web-Based Library at Baruch College Opens Doors." *College & Research Libraries News* 62 (5): 500–502.

Harwood, Doreen and Charlene McCormack. 2008. "Growing our Own: Mentoring Undergraduate Students." *Journal of Business & Finance Librarianship* 13 (3): 201–215.

Liao, Yan, Mary Finn, and Jun Lu. January 2007. "Information-Seeking Behavior of International Graduate Students Vs. American Graduate Students: A User Study at Virginia Tech 2005." *College & Research Libraries* 68 (1): 5–25.

Penn State University Division of Student Affairs. 2010. "New Students Fall 2010." Penn State University, http://studentaffairs.psu.edu/assessment/pdf/160.pdf.

Penn State University Libraries. 2010. "University Libraries Tours." Penn State University, http://www.libraries.psu.edu/psul/lls/outreach/tours.html.

Ross, Catherine Sheldrick. 1999. "Finding without Seeking: The Information

Encounter in the Context of Reading for Pleasure." *Information Processing & Management* 35 (6): 783–799. doi:10.1016/S0306-4573(99)00026-6.

Sanders, Mark. 2009. "Popular Reading Collections in Public University Libraries: A Survey of Three Southeastern States." *Public Services Quarterly* 5 (3): 174–183. doi:10.1080/15228950902976083.

Yi, Zhixian. 2007. "International Student Perceptions of Information Needs and use." *Journal of Academic Librarianship* 33 (6): 666–673. doi:10.1016/j.acalib.2007.09.003.

Chapter 5

International Education Week: Celebrating the Benefits of International Education and Exchange

Alena Aissing

> *"I've always believed that diplomacy does not just happen between government officials. It also happens between individuals through people to people connections. And student exchanges are some of the most important people to people connections we can have. For hundreds of thousands of students each year, exchanges promote mutual understanding and bring people of different nations together to share ideas and compare values. They also nurture leadership skills that prepare students for the challenges of the 21st century."*
> — Hillary Rodham Clinton (2010)

International Education Week (IEW) is a joint initiative of the U.S. Departments of State and Education; it was first held in 2000 and today is celebrated in more than 100 countries worldwide. It is an opportunity to celebrate the benefits of international education and student exchanges. This annual initiative aims to promote cross-cultural understanding and build support for international educational exchange by both encouraging the development of programs that prepare Americans to live and work in a global environment, and by also attracting future leaders from abroad to study in the United States. This chapter will describe initiatives and contributions of the University of Florida Libraries to the UF campus-wide IEW program. These activities sought to raise awareness and promote mutual understanding of diverse cultures during International Education Week, from November 15–19, 2010.

Introduction

International Education Week (IEW), held in November, has been celebrated in the United States and worldwide each year since President Bill Clinton instituted it in 2000. During IEW, colleges and universities across the country mobilize to highlight the important contributions of international education and exchange to the community and the nation by organizing special events, festivals, and other activities. One might ask why this recognition is important. It matters a great deal because, regardless of what students might do after graduation, they will be affected by the world beyond their borders. "Globalization" is a term used to describe this phenomenon. Globalization has many different definitions, but stripped to its essentials it means that ideas, goods and people are crossing international borders with greater impact, reach, speed and frequency than many would have thought possible a few years ago. Taking this into account and becoming aware of its problems and benefits has become an essential element in the educational process. To meet this need, the University of Florida Libraries, for the first time during fall 2010, planned and created an educational program and coordinated these activities together with the International Center.

The Institution

The University of Florida (UF) is a major, public, comprehensive, land-grant, and research university. The state's oldest and most comprehensive university, UF is among the nation's most academically diverse public universities. UF has a long history of established programs in international education, research and service. It is one of only 17 public, land-grant universities that belong to the Association of American Universities. UF traces its beginnings to a small seminary in 1853 and is now one of the largest universities in the United States, with more than 50,000 students. There are approximately 5,000 students from other countries studying at the University of Florida, which ranks 11th in the U.S. for hosting international students (Institute of International

Education 2011). For more information, please consult the UF homepage at http://www.ufl.edu.

The George A. Smathers Libraries

The George A. Smathers Libraries is a member of the Association of Research Libraries (ARL), the Center for Research Libraries (CRL), Association of Southeastern Research Libraries (ASERL), and LYRASIS. The library staff consists of more than 400 FTE librarians, technical/ clerical staff and student assistants. Special and Area Studies Collections encompass two units: the Area Studies Collections and the Special Collections of the University of Florida. The Area Studies Collections are the Latin American Collection, the Africana Collection, the Asian Studies Collection, and the Price Library of Judaica. Special Collections include Baldwin Library of Historical Children's Literature, the P.K. Yonge Library of Florida History, the General Manuscript Collection, the Harold and Mary Jean Hanson Rare Book Collection, the University Archives, the Architecture Archives, and the Popular Culture Collections.

University of Florida International Center (UFIC)

University of Florida has a long and distinguished tradition in international education and research in addition to a wide range of resources including faculty, staff and students with international interests. To respond to the rapidly changing global environment, the University of Florida established the UFIC in 1991. The UFIC serves as an internal and external liaison for the university, providing a source of assistance to faculty, administrators and students and enhancing their ability to pursue and develop international activities and initiatives. Among the primary services provided by UFIC are: International Speaker Series, International Curriculum Awards, Study Abroad Services, International Student Services, International Program Development, International Education Week (IEW), and Faculty and Scholar Services. UFIC also supports UF faculty and colleges in facilitation of international agreements.

The Initiatives

The First International Education Week Organized by the University of Florida Libraries: Building the Program

The development and enhancement of collaborative campus activities are part of the Libraries' outreach program, which aims to integrate the libraries' services, resources and collections, and subject expertise into all other academic programs and activities on campus. Creating the first library IEW program highlighted the importance of our libraries' educational role, participation and visibility in campus life.

In June of 2010, Alena Aissing, European Studies Librarian, approached Ms. Mabel Cardec, Coordinator for Outreach and Public Functions at the UFIC, to discuss a closer cooperation between the UFIC and the libraries. They initially met to plan developing instructional classes for graduate international students at the beginning of the Fall 2010 Semester. It was at this meeting, however, that Ms. Cardec asked Ms. Aissing if the libraries would be interested in contributing any library-related activities to the upcoming campus-wide IEW. This led to an energetic discussion of possible activities for which library and librarian participation would be beneficial to the IEW programming.

After this meeting, Ms. Aissing met with Dr. Isabel Silver, Director of Academic and Scholarly Outreach and Coordinator of the Library Instruction Committee, to develop a program plan that included various activities the libraries could provide, given the consideration of limited time available during the program and the desire to make the greatest impact. Dr. Silver approached the Library Instruction Committee with a list of possible ideas and activities for the Committee's input and participation, which led to greater teamwork and a coordinated effort. The members of the committee encouraged Alena Aissing to proceed with the development of the program and also volunteered their time for various activities.

Finally, Ms. Aissing approached librarians from different branch units, including the Humanities and Social Sciences branch (Library West), Area Studies, the Journalism Library, the Health Science Center, the Legal Information Center, and the public relations officer at the Libraries Administration Office. Library activities were incorporated into the campus-wide program, which also provided campus-wide publicity through the UF International Center as well as through the Libraries public relations officer. Because many librarians were willing to contribute their time and effort to IEW, we had fairly broad library participation for this first experience. The following examples describe the activities librarians provided.

International Education Week: Library Activities
From 'Commune' to International Community: A Writer's Journey from a Kibbutz Childhood to a Scholarly Life in Florida

The first library event offered was a presentation by Dr. Avraham Balaban, Professor of Modern Hebrew Literature in the Department of Languages, Literatures and Cultures at the University of Florida. Dr. Balaban received his Ph.D. from Tel Aviv University in 1979. In 1982 he won a prestigious Israeli literary prize, "The Prime Minister Creativity Award," for his two scholarly books and two books of poetry. Following his prize he was invited as a scholar and then as a visiting professor to Harvard University. He later served as an Assistant Professor of Modern Hebrew Literature at the University of Michigan (Ann Arbor) and came to UF in 1989.

Dr. Balaban's presentation, "From 'Commune' to International Community: a Writer's Journey from a Kibbutz Childhood to a Scholarly Life in Florida," explored both his creative writing and his scholarly work. He first presented a spellbinding description of his childhood on a kibbutz in Israel, and then read some passages from his 2004 memoir, *Mourning a Father Lost: A Kibbutz Childhood Remembered*. After discussing his latest scholarly book (2010), *Representations of Motherhood in Modern Hebrew Prose*, he finished the program by reading some lovely and beguiling poems from his latest collection, *Poems from a Foreign Place* (2010).

Participants informally shared with event organizers that they found Dr. Balaban's description of growing up as a child without parents in a communal setting and working together with other children on a farm captivating. During the presentation, the students, visitors and library staff were highly engaged and asked many questions. Participants wanted to know more about the communal values in a kibbutz, the lifestyles of its members and its impact on their families as well as influence of globalization leading to internal weakening of the commune. The presentation was extended from the planned forty minutes to one and half hour, due to participants' interest.

Reading Around the World

Hoping to construct cultural and historical bridges between the participants' lives and the words they read, and to introduce diverse cultures available through world literature, we designed a program called, "Reading around the World." The event was held in the Plaza of the Americas, a park in front of Library West. This was an invitation for students, faculty, staff and visitors to bring their favorite English translation of foreign poems, stories, novels, etc., to share with others by reading aloud.

During the "Reading around the World" event, participants talked about their choice of reading. Some of the readers told a story about how they first came across the book or story and how it influenced their decisions or directions in their lives. Simultaneously, these international stories and readings offered a unique opportunity to reach out to other students, including American students who might never have been exposed to travel or have had an experience of living in a foreign country.

Film Viewing of "A Day Without a Mexican"

On the third day of IEW, The George A. Smathers Library (East), Latin American Collection, lead by Richard Phillips, offered a viewing of the 2004 film, *A Day Without a Mexican* (*Día sin Mexicanos*), a Latin American "mockumentary" by Yarelli Arizmendi and Sergio Arau. In the film, a peculiar pink fog surrounds the state of California and communication outside its boundaries is completely closed off. As the day progresses, it becomes apparent that 14 million people have disappeared from the state, and the sole characteristic linking them is their Hispanic heritage.

Before and after viewing the film *A Day without a Mexican*, visitors had an opportunity to observe a special Mexican decoration. The Latin American Department created a "Mexican living room," with traditional fabrics, table cloth, pictures and decorative items such as dry corn hanging on the walls. While watching the movie, the participants felt like there were in a Mexican house. There was a brief discussion after the viewing, not only about the creation and meaning of the film, but also about the culture and the differences participants experienced while living on the University of Florida campus. Many of the students in the audience were from Latin America and shared the languages, history and culture of their home countries. They also shared how they dealt with culture shock during their first few weeks in the United States.

Traveling Exhibition: Darwin: Rewriting the Book of Nature

From the end of October through the beginning of December, the Health Science Center at the University of Florida hosted the National Library of Medicine's traveling exhibit, "Darwin: Rewriting the Book of Nature." For IEW, Michele Tennant, Health Science Center Libraries, used this exhibit to give an informal Galapagos Travelogue, "Rewriting the Book of Nature: Charles Darwin and the Rise of Evolutionary Theory."

Exhibition—Chinese Printing from Typeset to Digital Access

An ongoing exhibit, "Chinese Printing from Typeset to Digital Access," from the University of Florida Smathers Libraries Asian Studies Collections, showed various samples of Chinese print across the ages. David Hickey, Asian Studies Bibliographer, created a display of Smathers Libraries Special Collections and Library West materials related to Chinese printing, including an old-fashioned typeset, and samples of limited-issue modern print and digital production. On the top of the display cases were placed the current flyers and one stand-up poster for IEW so that, throughout the week, passers-by could learn about activities.

This exhibit was held in conjunction with a presentation titled, "Collecting and Reading in the Early Chinese Print Age," by Dr. Hilde De Weerdt from Oxford University. This event was co-sponsored by the Center for the Humanities and the Public Sphere at the University of Florida and Smathers Libraries.

Two Small Exhibitions: Miguel Hernandez and Mario Vargas Llosa

Other ongoing activities during the IEW were two exhibitions of award winning foreign authors at Library West, created by John Van Hook, Bibliographer for English Literature:

The first exhibition, on Spanish poet Miguel Hernandez, was mounted in support of a conference held at the University of Florida in the beginning of November. Since Hernandez was European, Leilani Freund, then Chair of Library West proposed that we extend the exhibit beyond the initial conference through IEW. The second exhibit that was organized in November, also by Dr. John Van Hook, concerned the works and life of Chilean author and 2004 Nobel Prize winner for Literature, Mario Vargas Llosa.

Global Art Exhibition

Also during the whole week, both the Education Library and Marston Science Library hosted a Global Art Exhibit from children in grades K-12. The public spaces at both libraries were filled with children's drawings and paintings that were submitted by students from several local schools. Their theme was, "children's imagination about foreign places," as well as their experiences with international films, books and travel.

Conclusion

The UF libraries' first experience in providing library related programs for IEW both demonstrated the Libraries' commitment to international education and reinforced the partnership now established with the UFIC. The proactive approach and successful cooperation between these academic units demonstrated organizational teamwork toward common goals: to serve UF's international students and show that the campus values their presence and contributions, and also to expose non-international students to other cultures. The libraries, as active members of the academic community, were critical to the success of this distinctive campus-wide and global education program. Such interactions, in turn, help employees of the libraries to understand the perspectives of various campus stakeholders and support new library partnerships.

Although the library program planners did not conduct a formal assessment of the program, informal feedback and observation shows that participants were engaged and enthusiastic about the UF libraries programs. There is now a commitment to future programming, and to make sure that timely planning, scheduling, and a wider variety of activities are included in the future IEW. We look forward to IEW 2011, and will consider new programs and any necessary modifications to last year's programming to increase participation and attendance at our events.

References

Balaban, Avraham. 2004. *Mourning a Father Lost: A Kibbutz Childhood Remembered*. Lanham MD: Rowman & Littlefield, 2004.

Balaban, Avraham. 2010. *Poems from a Foreign Place*. Ra anana, Israel: Even Hoshen Press.

Balaban, Avraham. 2010. *Representations of Motherhood in Modern Hebrew Prose*. Tel Aviv, Israel, Hakibbutz Hameuchad Publishing House Ltd.

Clinton, Hillary Rodham. 2010. "Video Remarks for International Education Week." (November 10, 2010). http://www.state.gov/secretary/rm/2010/11/150766.htm.

Chapter 6

Beyond the One-Shot Instruction Session: Semester-long Partnerships for International Student Success

Amy R. Hofer and Margot Hanson

Librarians at Golden Gate University are embedded in a program that helps acculturate international students to the American academic setting. This case study looks at how we developed an information literacy instruction curriculum that integrates with the program curriculum. We also look at strategies that we pursued to make our instruction efforts scalable as the program has grown. Librarians providing in-depth information literacy instruction to the program have made great strides in development of flexible campus partnerships, learning assessment, and student outreach.

Introduction

Instruction librarians are always looking for ways to connect with students where they are, and in most cases that means the classroom. In the absence of an information literacy credit course, librarian access often depends on invitations from faculty. At Golden Gate University (GGU), librarians' outreach efforts result in an average of 40 one-shot instruction sessions per semester, usually about 45 minutes long, where we do our best to be engaging and hope that students will call, email, or visit us to follow up on what we have introduced in our allotted time. We also offer webinars and visit online discussion boards to lead discussions on research topics and sources.

Yet this model is problematic because it relies on "academic champions"—that is, faculty who make a point of including information literacy and librarians in their classes. Librarians are not in a strong position if we have to depend on the continuing hospitality of individual faculty members. Further, ad hoc cooperation doesn't enable us to do strategic or long-term planning (McGuinness 2007). Information literacy embedded in the curriculum at the programmatic or institutional level is not only more sustainable but also gives us the opportunity to teach more effectively and in greater depth (Johnston and Webber 2003).

With the aim of going beyond the one-shot instruction session, GGU librarians successfully collaborated with a program dedicated to international students to embed library instruction in the program curriculum. As the working relationship has evolved, librarians have been able to provide input on assignments, suggest appropriate reading materials, and have a voice in curriculum-level planning. This partnership has contributed to international student success and taken the University Library's instruction program in exciting new directions.

The Institution

Located in the heart of downtown San Francisco, Golden Gate University (GGU) offers a variety of business and professional graduate degrees for a primarily nontraditional student body. The student makeup is the reverse of most schools, with the undergraduate population in the hundreds and the graduate population in the thousands. GGU attracts a significant number of international students, and librarians work with these students not only within the context of their regular classes, but also in an immersion program for provisionally admitted international students. In keeping with national trends (Institute of International Education 2010), China and Taiwan are leading countries of origin for students in this program, but we also work with many Middle Eastern, South and Southeast Asian, and Eastern European students (Simeonova 2011).

The immersion program, called Preparation in Language and University Studies (PLUS), offers international applicants with TOEFL scores below the requirement for regular admission to GGU an intensive semester of language and academic skill-building. Successful completion of the PLUS program gains students admittance to a mainstream GGU program. The PLUS curriculum includes four different courses, which are carefully designed to mutually reinforce the learning objectives for the program. For example, the company research that students do for their Academic Communication Skills PowerPoint presentation assignment will be used again for another assignment in the Applied Critical Thinking course. The curriculum design team members—made up of PLUS program administrators and instructors—are experienced collaborators and communicators; these qualities are a hallmark of the department culture.

When Hofer arrived at GGU in 2008 as Research Instruction Librarian, the University Library already had a positive relationship with the PLUS department and librarians were frequently invited to PLUS classes. By the time Hanson came to GGU in 2009 as Web Services Librarian, the PLUS program was beginning its growth phase and there was an expectation that librarians would visit classes approximately 8 times per semester to support research assignments. Hofer's successor arrived in Fall 2010, at the peak of PLUS enrollment, and has continued the efforts towards a model of advance planning and team teaching in order to handle the load.

The Initiative
Logistics
In order to meet the expectations of the PLUS department, we need to develop our plans for library instruction at the same time that PLUS develops their curriculum. Starting the conversation early has been a necessary reminder to the PLUS administrators—who have tremendously heavy workloads and many demands on their time—to consult with us as they plan their assignments and lessons. Often the conversa-

Figure 6.1: Short learning objects embedded in the PLUS LibGuide, http://ggu.libguides.com/plus

tion can be initiated on the basis of a scheduling request: "This is what we did with you this semester, shall we look at dates for next semester?" Reserving time in our instruction schedule also helps us plan for the inevitable flurry of requests from other departments during the first month of the term.

PLUS instructors have generously educated librarians on providing instruction to English Language Learners, with tips such as slowing down, allowing pauses after questions, and rephrasing

Figure 6.2: SWOT analysis review on the PLUS LibGuide, http://ggu. libguides.com/plus

information in a few different ways. We discovered that another crucial element for English Language Learners is receiving information in multiple modes, so we incorporate repetition into our lesson planning. For example, librarians and PLUS section leaders help students keep up during lecture/demos; librarians circulate during lab time to assist individual students with the research skill of the day; and the PLUS LibGuide allows students to access instructional content outside of class time. Figure 6.1 illustrates short videos on topic development embedded in the PLUS LibGuide and assigned as homework before class, while Figure 6.2 shows a LibGuide review of the SWOT Analysis (Strengths, Weaknesses, Opportunities, Threats) lesson for reference after class. If students need yet another pass at the material we plan for in-person visits to the reference desk or librarian's office.

Building repetition into our lesson plans became more challenging as PLUS enrollment has nearly doubled between 2008–2010, far outpacing growth in both overall University enrollment and the international student body (see Table 6.1) (Baba 2010). We passed an important scalability milestone when the program grew bigger than the maximum capacity of GGU's largest computer lab. One solution was to split the group in half and offer lecture/demos in back-to-back shifts. A more recent modification is to teach twice as many classes on consecutive days, incorporating lab time into lecture/demo sessions instead of having librarians come back and facilitate dedicated lab sessions.

Table 6.1: Fall term enrollment figures for the GGU student population, international student enrollment, and the PLUS program, 2007–2010.

	GGU	% change	International	% change	PLUS	% change
Fall 2007	2,670		400		34	
Fall 2008	2,635	–1.3	480	20	28	–17.6
Fall 2009	2,756	4.6	530	10.4	44	57.1
Fall 2010	2,879	4.5	600	13.2	53	20.5

Perhaps the biggest lesson learned was that for the embedded librarian model to work smoothly, we had to stop planning on an ad hoc basis so that the instruction librarian could be assured of a team-teaching partner during class visits, and so that the rest of the library's instruction program could be planned around the significant preparation and commitment that these visits entailed. Appendices A and B show examples of planning documents we have created during different semesters and shared with the PLUS team. Advance planning helps librarians find creative ways to balance PLUS instruction with other workload demands.

Learning Objectives

The PLUS instructors initially invited us to classes in order to help with skill building for specific research tasks, but over time we have been able to establish information literacy learning objectives as well. Some of these objectives, such as ethical and critical use of source material, are already incorporated into the objectives of the PLUS program. An additional objective that we have for PLUS is orienting students to several of the top sources for the basic types of research that students will be doing in the rest of their studies at GGU.

We try to help students experience success with finding the information they need using the library databases so that they will return to these sources when they leave the PLUS program for mainstream classes. While the librarians want to ensure the students' success, we hesitate to spoon-feed the answers to them. However, when working with PLUS students we often find that business research is very challenging, even though we provide them with exactly what they need. We find ourselves offering more explicit guidance than we might to other student groups, in order to provide as clear an example as possible of successfully completing research tasks. Our lessons are planned with this objective in mind, and we have worked with PLUS to guide assignments towards alignment with this objective.

We learned early on how surprisingly difficult this can be. For example, when teaching to an assignment where students were asked to create presentations on whether their company should expand to a new country, we discovered (during our lab visit) that some of the companies assigned were multinationals that already operate in almost every single country on the globe, such as Coca-Cola and United Parcel Service (UPS). This kind of assignment is great for practicing country research and taking a position on an issue, but using last-resort sources to scrape up market data for tiny countries doesn't meet the objective of the assignment, from our perspective—that is, learning how to use the obvious "go-to" sources for country research such as the Economist Intelligence Unit or Euromonitor. Several students during that term were stuck with unfortunate combinations of companies and countries for their projects.

The interconnected design of the PLUS curriculum is a great strength of the program, but also makes planning extremely complex because a change to one assignment can have reverberations in all of the classes. To carry forward the example, if we are using the country research assignment in the future then we should assign only companies that do not already operate in all of the countries for which we have Consumer Lifestyles reports from Euromonitor. (Netflix is a good example of an interesting company that only operated in North America during the semester that a student was assigned this company.) At the same time, however, we also want students to learn how to use the library's obvious "go-to" sources for *company* research, such as Mergent Online, OneSource, and DataMonitor reports via Business Source Complete. So companies must also be public and large enough to have profiles in these sources.

The first semester after we realized how all the pieces of the puzzle fit together, Hofer did the legwork to vet companies and countries for the PLUS program. As the PLUS curriculum designers became aware of what was needed, they have moved to checking the availability of research sources for themselves. By training the trainers we have made the library's resources more central to the PLUS planning process and enabled the PLUS instructional faculty to become power users themselves. As this scenario illustrates, though, clarity about learning objectives is only the first step to seeing those objectives met.

Lesson Planning: Topic Development

Since librarians work closely with the PLUS instructors at a curricular level, we are able to focus on concepts and skills relevant to what students are working on that week. Librarians offer instruction around PLUS assignments that require students to conduct company, industry, and country research, create SWOT analyses, and write a research paper. We help students find appropriate sources and then encourage students to use those sources to do their own analysis. Each time we teach a lesson, we consider changes for the next time based on student observation and feedback from PLUS instructors.

An area of perennial difficulty is topic development for the research paper, so we will look at that lesson for our case study. Although librarians and PLUS instructors dedicate quite a bit of time to this important skill, many final papers each term are essentially data dumps rather than papers asking a question of an appropriate scope to delve into a meaty topic for 10 pages. The difficulty of this area for the students was borne out by our assessment results, discussed in the next section.

One problem that librarians have identified with student research questions is the common tendency toward a one-size-fits-all topic that is not specific to the company or industry: How can my company be number one? How can my company recover from the bad economy? Getting the students to stop searching and read what they have found is another struggle: once they start searching, they want to keep going interminably rather than moving onto the next steps of reading, analyzing, evaluating, and ultimately, writing. We also observe the belief (common to many students who grew up with the Internet) that the perfect report or article exists that will answer their research question. In short, students think that someone has already written their paper and they just have to find it—a sure sign that they have not yet grasped that research papers look at questions that we *don't* already know all the answers to.

Guiding students through the process of brainstorming possible topics, narrowing their focus, and then developing strategies to find relevant sources is an area of library involvement that is evolving on a semester-by-semester basis through continued experimentation with different instruction approaches. For example, rather than simply asking students to brainstorm based on their previous research about their company, the brainstorming session now includes walking through an example with the whole class, using a current business event as an example. One semester we used BP as the example, and asked students to think through the "5 W's" (who, what, when, where, and why) related to the 2010 Gulf of Mexico oil spill. Another event, closer to home, was the Pacific Gas & Electric gas line explosion in San Bruno, CA. After this practice, the students are expected to apply the brainstorming technique to the company they are researching.

The class on evaluating student research questions has evolved from a whole-class discussion to small-group work. In the past, students each wrote several potential research questions on the board, and the librarian led the class in determining together which question was best. The new activity focuses on peer evaluation of possible paper topics, using a worksheet developed by PLUS instructors to help students classify questions as too broad, too narrow, or just right (after a very abridged telling of "Goldilocks and the Three Bears," which our students have never heard before).

For the upcoming semester, librarians and PLUS instructors plan to try a concept mapping exercise in order to relate the students' company research to their personal interests. In the past we have verbally suggested to students that they pursue a topic that interests them. The new exercise will help students make their own connections by laying out mind-map bubbles for company information, industry information, professional interests, and personal interests. Each student will make an appointment with a librarian to go over the brainstorming sheet and look for possible intersections between personal interests and research topics. Students will take away search strategies and a few articles to start their literature reviews, leading toward a refined research question for the final paper. Appendices C and D are examples of handouts for topic development lessons.

Assessment

Achieving embedded information literacy instruction in a GGU program is the exception, not the rule. Despite an observed need, the culture of GGU tends to be lukewarm towards information literacy initiatives beyond the library's doors. We decided to leverage our success with the PLUS program into an assessment study that could produce data persuasive enough to gain organizational cooperation for a more strategic information literacy instruction program at GGU. Conducting assessment also helped us confirm our observations about what was working and where we might improve our instruction in the PLUS program.

Drawing on the support and expertise of GGU's Director of Assessment and Evaluation, we conducted a mixed-methods study (Hofer and Hanson 2010). The first phase of the study was an anonymous quiz that was given to PLUS students at the beginning and end of the semester. The quiz was also given to a control group of undergraduates who did not receive any library instruction that term. The quiz assessed students on information literacy topics that we teach in PLUS: source evaluation, topic development, citation, and library use.

We found that the difference between the PLUS pre- and post-test scores was statistically significant (Kramer 2010). This finding indicates to us that our intensive intervention is justified by a measurable impact on student learning. It is important for our department to know that the data supports continuing to invest staff time and resources in PLUS instruction.

We are not able to use our data to claim that our intervention was so effective that the PLUS students, who start at a disadvantage because of their language skills, are boosted above the level of the undergraduates receiving little or no library instruction (that is, the difference between the PLUS post-test and the undergraduate quiz scores was not statistically significant). However, it is worth noting that almost half of the undergraduate group consisted of English Language Learners who passed the TOEFL for regular admittance to GGU, and that this group had lower quiz scores than the native English speakers. We hypothesize that English Language Learners at GGU, in general, may need more information literacy instruction than the native speakers, but since PLUS students represent less than 10% of GGU's international student body we are missing many more English Language Learners than we are reaching. Figure 6.3 summarizes the data from the quiz responses.

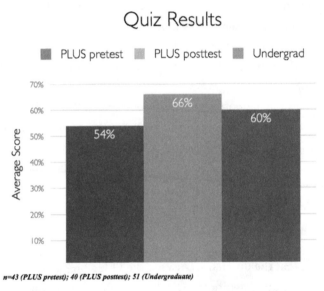

n=43 (PLUS pretest); 40 (PLUS posttest); 51 (Undergraduate)

Figure 6.3: Quiz scores for PLUS pretest, PLUS posttest, and Undergraduates.

For the second phase of the study, we conducted a systematic examination of PLUS final papers using a rubric (see Appendix E) to look at whether students were able to apply their skills in three areas that we taught to during the semester: use of appropriate sources, topic development, and citation. We found that while a majority of students demonstrated an acceptable understanding of appropriate sources and citation, students remained weak on topic development despite considerable effort spent on instruction (Figure 6.4 summarizes the data from the work samples). As we describe in the section above, we continually refine how we teach topic development because it is so challenging for students. The PLUS curriculum designers concur that topic development remains a problem and have also made adjustments to the research paper assignment.

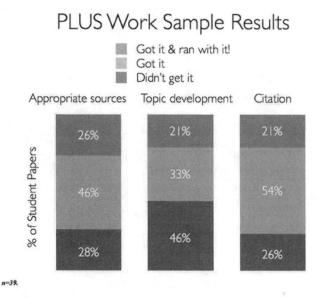

Figure 6.4: Student paper scores.

One gratifying finding of the study was the discovery that our instruction program provides highly effective outreach. On our quiz, we asked students to self-report about whether they value the library and its services. Only about half of the undergraduates agreed with this sentiment, which correlates with their self-reporting on whether they use the library for research help. On the other hand, by the end of the semester PLUS students overwhelmingly said that the library contributes to their academic success at GGU (see Figure 6.5). This data suggests that from an outreach perspective the PLUS intervention is wildly successful. Further, after one semester, these students will bring their positive perception of the library into their mainstream GGU classes, their small group work, and other word-of-mouth relationships, so that PLUS students become ambassadors for the library.

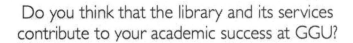

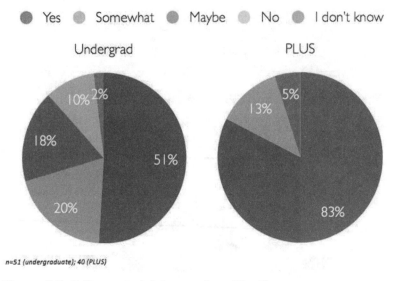

n=51 (undergraduate); 40 (PLUS)

Figure 6.5: Self-reported data on value of the library.

Looking Ahead

We expect that we will continue to tinker with our lessons and delivery methods as long as we continue working with PLUS. For example, in Spring 2011 we will be piloting a new model of individual appointments with librarians to develop research paper topics and begin literature reviews. This could prove to be more effective, or completely overwhelming in terms of librarian-hours invested. Looking even farther ahead, we might try group appointments in order to reach a few students at once and help students overcome possible shyness or intimidation they could feel during individual appointments.

As the collaboration between PLUS and the library moves forward, we also continue to work on balancing the needs of PLUS students with other demands on librarians' time. The question of whether the current model is sustainable will have to be revisited on a regular basis, particularly if PLUS enrollment remains steady or continues to grow. The expansion of other programs in the university as well as the addition of new programs put additional strain on the time of librarians providing research instruction in multiple departments. The PLUS administrators view our support as so essential that they are clamoring for an additional librarian position to meet the program's growing needs.

Conclusion

We read case studies because others' scenarios and problem solving can spark new ideas in our own work. We also look for themes that might be generalized to other settings. The PLUS collaboration is unusual in that we began with extended access to a cohort of students and had a highly process-oriented department to work with. The culture of that department is open to continually revising content, and is not territorial about sharing that process with outsiders. We also had a significant head start in conducting assessment in that we were able to work with an extremely helpful University-wide assessment coordinator (Oakleaf and Hinchliffe 2010). Still, we hope that some of our experience can be used in any setting.

In particular, the PLUS collaboration demonstrates the importance of embedded instruction rather than relying on ad hoc access to departments through the more common "academic champions" model. PLUS library instruction has withstood staff turnover in both the library and in PLUS and we have achieved measurable success with student learning. On a personal level, we enjoy getting to know the students and observing their growth over the term. With resources always at a premium in libraries, it is a strategic choice to prioritize substantive learning over greater quantities of one-shot orientation sessions.

As for replicating the success of this model at another institution, or even sustaining the program at GGU, the key element has proven to be flexibility. In this we were fortunate to have the PLUS team model willingness to question, improve, and change as needed. Working with the diversity of international students in PLUS helps us stay on our toes and strengthens the Library's entire Instruction Program.

Acknowledgements

Special thanks to Josephine Tam for her assistance and Janice Carter for her support.

References

Baba, Toshie (Associate Director of International Admissions and Advising, Golden Gate University). E-mail message to author. (December 17, 2010).

Hofer, Amy R. and Margot Hanson. 2010. "Upstairs-downstairs: Working with a campus assessment coordinator and other allies for effective information literacy assessment." In *CARL 2010 Proceedings*, Sacramento CA, April 8–10, 2010. http://carl-acrl.org/Archives/ConferencesArchive/Conference10/proceedings.html.

Institute of International Education. 2010. "*Open Doors* 2010 Fast Facts." Open Doors. http://www.iie.org/en/research-and-publications/~/media/Files/Corporate/Open-Doors/Fast-Facts/Fast%20Facts%202010.ashx.

Johnston, Bill, and Sheila Webber. 2003. "Information Literacy in Higher Education: A Review and Case Study." *Studies in Higher Education* 28 (3): 335–353.

Kramer, Lisa (Director of Assessment and Evaluation, Golden Gate University). E-mail message to author. (May 25, 2010).

McGuinness, Claire. 2007. "Exploring Strategies for Integrated Information Literacy: From 'Academic Champions' to Institution-Wide Change." *Communications in Information Literacy* 1 (1): 26–38.

Oakleaf, Megan, and Lisa Hinchliffe. 2010. "Assessment cycle or circular file: Do academic librarians use information literacy assessment data?" In *Proceedings of the 2008 Library Assessment Conference*, Seattle WA, August 4–7, 2010. http://libraryassessment.org/bm~doc/proceedings-lac-2008.pdf.

Simeonova, Maria (Program Coordinator, PLUS Program, Golden Gate University). E-mail message to author. (January 19, 2011).

Appendix A: PLUS semester timeline, Summer 2010.

Critical Thinking class visits are in normal font and Case Study class visits are in *italics*.

Week	Date	Assignment/ Activity	Librarian Lesson
3	*Tues. May 18, 10:45–12*	*Country research—study questions (case study)*	*EIU, GMID consumer profiles, country research online guide*
7	*Thurs. June 17, 10:45–12*	*Global positioning*	*Company research*
8	Mon. June 28, 11–12	Topic development— Research paper (critical thinking)	Goldilocks, 5 W's, advanced search, one-minute methods of topic development; OneSource for company information and news; 1:1 identify possible topics
8	*Tues. June 22, 9:20–12*	*Industry research—Global positioning presentation (case study)*	*GMID industry profiles, OneSource for Datamonitor industry reports (bonus: IBIS for US & China), Review country research*
8	Wed. June 30, 10:50–12	Article searching— Research paper	Getting from question to database search, brainstorming keywords from reading, ABI & BSC
9	Wed. July 7, 11–12	Article searching— Research paper	1:1 help finding sources needed (articles, reports, profiles, etc)
9	*Thurs. July 1, 10:45–12*	*SWOT analysis*	*DataMonitor company reports in BSC, S&P "How To Analyze" reports, Company/org menu choice in ABI; 1:1 help*
10	*Tues. July 6, 10:45–12*	*SWOT—follow-up visit*	*1:1 search help*

Appendix B: PLUS semester timeline, Spring 2011

Date	Activity	Lesson
Jan. 20	Country Research	GMID and EIU
Feb. 8	Company Research	OneSource (including Annual Reports) and Mergent Online
Feb. 15	SWOT Research	Business Source Complete SWOT for keywords and then Proquest for articles using those keywords
Feb. 22	Industry Research	IBIS and DataMonitor industry reports in Business Source Complete
Feb. 28–March 14	Topic Development	30-minute individual appointments with students about their "Brainstorming Bubbles" for research topics. After appointments, students will do a literature review on their own and then create research questions.

Appendix C: PLUS topic development handout, Spring 2009.

PLUS/TOPIC DEVELOPMENT   SPRING 2009

Academic Communication Skills: Library Resources

University Library

http://www.ggu.edu/university_library/

Topic development: Find an angle

The Goldilocks approach: Not too broad, not too narrow, but *juuuust right*.

The 5 W's approach: *Narrow* your topic by thinking about Who, What, When, Where, and Why.

The Advanced Search approach: Searches with one term answer "what is...?" type questions. Searches with at least two terms answer more complex questions that you can *take a position on*.

The 1-minute approach: You have a good working knowledge of your topic when you can talk for *an entire minute* without stopping.

Finding background information (*before* you look for articles)

Gale Virtual Reference Library provides online access to three great industry encyclopedias. Reference sources (print and electronic) give you an overview on your topic and links to more research sources.

Company and Industry profiles provide a lot of background information. Check databases such as **OneSource, S&P NetAdvantage, & IBISWorld** for financial data for companies, industry reports, and market research, ratios, statistics, news, and analysis.

On the web: You can find good information to get started by checking a company's website, Wikipedia, and Yahoo! Finance. Make sure to *carefully evaluate* any information you find on the web!

Can't find what you need? Ask a librarian!

Amy Hofer | (415) 442-7251 | ahofer@ggu.edu

Appendix D: PLUS topic development handout, Spring 2011.

Created by Karen McRobie, Natalia Barbera, Suzy Bausch, and Linda Koza.

PLUS at Golden Gate University   **Applied Critical Thinking**

Directions: Fill out this form with your own interests; then, meet with a university librarian or your PLUS instructor to help you create possible subtopics to research.

Name: _____   Degree Program: _____

My clubs
_____
_____

My hobbies
_____
_____

My brands/products
_____
_____
_____

Company: _____
Strengths:
_____
_____
Weaknesses:
_____
_____
In the news:
_____
_____
_____

My dream Job
_____
_____

My Country:
_____
In the news:
_____
_____
_____

Environmental Concerns
_____
_____

Industry: _____
Opportunities:
_____
Threats:
_____
In the news:
_____
_____
_____

My social networks
_____
_____

Humanitarian Concerns
_____
_____

Other: _____
_____
_____

Other: _____
_____
_____

My travels
_____
_____

Economic Concerns
_____
_____

Possible Subtopics:
1. _____
2. _____
3. _____

Appendix E: Rubric for scoring research papers.

	Didn't Get It	Got It	Got It & Ran With It!
A: Appropriate Sources	• Uses only one format • Not relevant or authoritative • Heavy reliance on one or two sources	• Uses a range of formats, including reports, articles and websites • Uses only resources presented in class	• Uses a range of formats, including reports, articles and websites • Includes resources only available from the library, but went beyond resources presented in class • Sources are relevant and substantive
B: Topic Development	• Topic too narrow or too broad for assignment • Uses report format, as a simple statement of facts, missing original analysis	• Research question is of appropriate scope for assignment • Includes original analysis • Question can be answered with resources presented in class	• Uses critical thinking and creative approach to topic, which is of appropriate scope • Research question requires original analysis • Question requires additional sources beyond what was presented in class
C: Citation	• Errors in APA formatting • Incorrect use of paraphrasing, quotations, or summarizing • Quotes are dumped into paper and not incorporated into analysis • Originality report reveals problems with exact matches	• Consistent APA formatting in-text and reference list • Originality report reveals less than 10% exact match	• APA correctly and consistently used for in-text and reference list citations • Citations are distributed evenly throughout paper, contribute to analysis, and support conclusions

Chapter 7

A Multifaceted Model of Outreach and Instruction for International Students

Merinda Kaye Hensley and Emily Love

A multifaceted library outreach and instruction program consists of six elements: staff development, partnerships, outreach, instruction, student needs, and assessment. This chapter considers the varied academic needs of international students as they transition to a new campus community in a different language and encourages library faculty and staff to build upon the distinct benefits of a diverse campus community. The University of Illinois has developed a holistic model that builds on the strengths of librarians, staff, campus partners, as well as international students.

Introduction

In 2006, librarians at the University of Illinois at Urbana-Champaign embarked on creating a versatile multicultural outreach program that would extend library services and instruction beyond the traditional classroom experience by building staff training and campus partnerships. International student enrollment continues to rise on the University of Illinois at Urbana-Champaign campus, currently second in international student enrollment at public universities according to the 2009/2010 Open Doors Report (Institute of International Education 2010). The Outreach Librarian for Multicultural Services and the Instructional Services Librarian strategically developed a multifaceted model of outreach and instruction that incorporates six primary components: staff development, partnerships, outreach, instruction, student needs, and assessment (Figure 7.1). This initiative considers the varied academic needs of international students as they transition to a new campus community in a different language while encouraging library faculty and staff to build upon the distinct benefits of a diverse campus community. The following case study is a vision of multicultural services that outlines and provides examples of a programmatic model designed to be modified to fit a variety of institutional types.

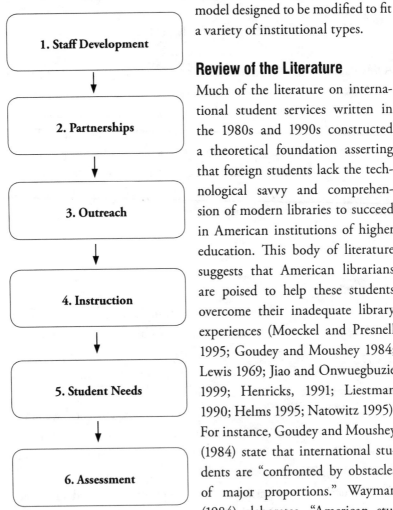

Figure 7.1: A multifaceted model of outreach and instruction for international students.

Review of the Literature

Much of the literature on international student services written in the 1980s and 1990s constructed a theoretical foundation asserting that foreign students lack the technological savvy and comprehension of modern libraries to succeed in American institutions of higher education. This body of literature suggests that American librarians are poised to help these students overcome their inadequate library experiences (Moeckel and Presnell 1995; Goudey and Moushey 1984; Lewis 1969; Jiao and Onwuegbuzie 1999; Henricks, 1991; Liestman 1990; Helms 1995; Natowitz 1995). For instance, Goudey and Moushey (1984) state that international students are "confronted by obstacles of major proportions." Wayman (1984) elaborates, "American students are taught to be self-sufficient in a library. They must use the card catalog, retrieve their own books, check them out, and carry them back to their rooms. This idea of self-service is an anathema to some foreign students…" Liestman (1990) comments, "Most students are accustomed to rote learning rather than research. Independent study is rare."

A number of outreach practices and instructional programs are discussed in studies of international students; however, Conteh-Morgan (2003) argues that there are entrenched beliefs regarding international students that construct a mental model where librarians base their services on the idea that international students are "flat, non-evolving characters, continually laboring under the weight of linguistic, cultural, and technological disadvantages as they try to acquire an American education." Librarians can go beyond relying on outdated research and focus instead on establishing connections with campus partners to determine international students' needs when developing new programs and initiatives.

The Institution

The University of Illinois at Urbana-Champaign, the state's flagship and oldest public university currently enrolls over 43,000 students in more than 150 fields of study. According to the Institute for International Education's 2010 Open Doors Report, 7,287 international students from 119 countries elected to study at the University of Illinois during the 2009/2010 academic year. The percentage of international student attendance at Illinois has increased dramatically from 11.38 percent of the student population in 2001/2002 to 16.67 percent in 2009/2010. Students' places of origin mirror the rest of the country, with almost half of all international students coming from China, India and South Korea. In both undergraduate and graduate student enrollment, the University of Illinois' Student Data Book indicates that Engineering and Business and Management are the most popular disciplines among international students. The campus also ranks second in the nation's top 40 Doctoral/Research institutions in the number of international students according to the most recent Open Doors Report.

The Initiatives

First level—Staff development

Staff training and development for librarians, library staff and student workers is a key component toward fostering a culturally competent environment on campus. Training programs can often be developed through collaborations with other academic departments and student services units as a means to address new topics and areas of interest.

Library Diversity Committee

The Illinois Library Diversity Committee provides leadership and guidance to the library faculty and staff by encouraging awareness about and discussions on diversity. Specifically, the committee focuses on diversity issues with regard to library climate, cultural competence in the workplace, staff training and development, services to patrons, and campus outreach. The Diversity Committee also constructed the Library Diversity Statement with input from the entire library staff as a way to demonstrate commitment to supporting diverse students, faculty, and staff members:

> The University of Illinois Library is committed to an environment that welcomes, cultivates, values, respects and supports the differences and contributions of all students, faculty and staff at the University of Illinois, and the community. In addition, the University Library is dedicated to creating an inclusive community grounded in respect and appreciation for all individuals who work in the library. The library recognizes diversity as a constantly changing concept. It is purposefully defined broadly as encompassing, but not limited to, individuals' social, cultural, mental and physical differences. (http://www.library.illinois.edu/committee/diversity/charge.html)

Staff Training

Library and staff training remains a pivotal component in the facilitation of establishing effective public service and communication with international students. The librarians partner with faculty and staff in other academic departments and student affairs offices such as the School of Social Work, the Office of Equal Opportunity and Access, and the Office of International Programs to provide training programs for librarians and staff working in public service positions. Through these partnerships, the Library's Diversity Committee sponsors an annual staff training program that reflects the library's commitment to inclusion and cultural competence. Past programs include:

- Training on microaggressions led by a faculty member from the School of Labor and Employment Relations
- Sessions on inclusion in the workplace conducted by the Office of Inclusion and Intercultural Relations
- Workshops on cultural competence in libraries led by faculty members in the School of Social Work

The Library Diversity Committee also hosts regular 'snack breaks' for the library's staff, which serve as a facilitated discussion on current topics. Additionally, the library encourages faculty and staff to seek out learning experiences that foster a climate of civility and inclusion. The library's unique partnership with the Mortenson Center for International Library Programs (http://www.library.illinois.edu/mortenson/) offers librarians opportunities to mentor and learn from international librarians as a way to understand not only other cultures, but to also learn about libraries in other areas of the world.

Second Level—Partnerships
Finding and establishing partnerships with student affairs units serving international students is a key step towards identifying, developing and sustaining new library programs and services for international students. Librarians can consider establishing relationships beyond faculty partners to include international student affairs units in order to facilitate students' access to the library's services, programs, collections and expertise. Love and Edwards (2009) suggest that the key to devel-

oping successful partnerships is recognizing the specific and unique needs of international students while "understanding the information component of these needs and seeking out collaborators to assist us in addressing those needs."

Partnerships developed between the library and Illinois campus offices serving international students include the Office of International Students and Scholars Services, the Intensive English Institute, the Department of Linguistic's English as a Second Language Program, the Study Abroad Office and the four Cultural Centers. These partnerships are integral to the development of outreach initiatives and programs designed to reach international students, visiting international scholars, and their families on campus, since they help to identify unmet student needs that inform new programs and services for international students. These collaborations and partnerships also generate new marketing opportunities for the library's programs and services for international students. Additionally, staff members at these offices may possess academic backgrounds and expert knowledge of cross-cultural communication methods, which can help to identify additional projects, lead to new collaborations, and the development of valuable training programs for librarians and library staff working in public services positions. For instance, staff members at the Illinois Office of International Students and Scholars hold a series of training programs designed to help faculty and staff to learn more about international students' backgrounds and cultures.

Third Level—Outreach

Outreach to students beyond their traditional library experiences extends the library's services and programs to facilitate students' access to the library's services, programs, collections, and research assistance whether online, in other physical locations, or at the library.

International Student Orientations

Each fall and spring semester, the International Students and Scholars Services (ISSS), offers a new international student orientation for which the Outreach Librarian for Multicultural Services designs and delivers information about the library's services, programs and collections. New international students attend this daylong orientation program with presentations from campus services such as financial services, athletic programs, campus safety and the library. These orientations also connect students to a librarian, giving them an immediate contact for referrals for future research assistance. The fall orientations are conveniently scheduled one week prior to the library's annual multilingual series of building tours, which helps to increase marketing and promotion. The orientations serve as an invaluable venue to distribute library information including promotional material, library guides and handouts. There are plans to develop materials in languages other than English.

Multilingual Library Tours

The University Library initiated an annual series of multilingual library tours in 2005, held at the start of each fall semester. The tours are designed to bring together library staff, new students, researchers and their families. The first year the library offered tours, twenty-eight students and community members attended, and by the fifth year, the number rose slightly to thirty-five. Results from an initial survey highlight that graduate students and their families compose the majority of attendees. A 2008 University of Illinois graduate student's thesis (Shiflet 2008) observed that non-native-English-speaking spouses, classified as dependents on their full-time graduate student's spouse visa, often face more obstacles finding a place in the community. The study shows that the library stood out as a milieu that offers dependent visa holders a place of support and inclusion. Participants in the study, mostly women, agreed that they appreciated exposure to collections in their native languages in addition to a friendly face that they could connect with in the future.

The combination of recruitment, training and publicity are critical elements in developing a series of multilingual tours. First, library staff volunteers are recruited through the library-wide email distribution list. Following recruitment, tour leaders attend a 30-minute training session where they receive a script of the tour in English, which they are responsible for translating. Posters are used to publicize the tour schedule throughout the library and on campus. Over the past four years, library staff, librarians, and graduate student assistants have led tours in an array of languages that include French, German, Thai, Japanese, Chinese, Hindi, Punjabi, Urdu, Arabic, Turkish, Spanish, Swahili, Polish and Russian.

Feedback from the volunteer tour leaders indicates their interest in the opportunity to speak with new campus community members in their native language. The multilingual tours, particularly those led in Korean, Chinese, Japanese and Swahili are well attended. The tours help to extend immersion opportunities to university students studying new languages. Finally, the tours increase an overall sense of inclusion among library employees. Multilingual tours require no additional funding, only staff time, and can be easily replicable depending on an institution's strength of existing partnerships with international programs and the number of staff with multilingual backgrounds.

Reaching out to international students in multiple formats allows the student to choose what puts them at ease. For library tours, formats include cell phone tours, virtual tours and self-paced audio tours. For example, Illinois translated an audio tour into Chinese in order to accommodate the large number of Chinese students on campus.

Marketing Strategies

Marketing remains a linchpin in the process of attracting students to the library's programs and services. The University of Illinois librarians rely on several primary methods of communication to promote and market the library's programs. Libraries can publicize events and programs through a variety of mediums, including email distribution lists and posters or flyers in the following locations:

- The Office of International Students and Scholars
- New Orientation Programs for International Students
- The Study Abroad Office

- Faculty and Staff email distribution lists campus-wide
- Foreign Language Departments
- The English Institutes and English Language Schools in the Community
- The Student Union and other public student venues
- Family and International Student Housing
- The library's website

International student programs serve as valuable promotional partners, as they can disseminate information and publicity to their student email distribution lists, reaching thousands of students. When developing instructional programs, film events, tours and orientations, marketing serves not only the international students, but all faculty, staff, students, and community members, helping to establish a more robust campus experience for everyone.

Fourth Level—Instruction

Recent literature documents common struggles that international students face in conducting research at U.S. academic libraries including language barriers, familiarity with library systems, general cultural adjustments, as well as research and writing skills. (Badke 2002; Baron & Strout-Dapaz 2001). Parallel to the ways in which information literacy has been incorporated into undergraduate education, librarians can assist in untangling the complex information needs of international students.

Course-integrated Instruction

Course-integrated instruction provides the librarian with an opportunity to work with international students within the context of an assigned research project. Students who enter the University of Illinois who do not speak English as their first language and have not met the mandated score for the Test of English as a Foreign Language (TOEFL) exam must take an ESL Placement Test (EPT). The EPT determines who is required to take English as a Second Language (ESL) courses as part of their academic degree. In response, the library built a partnership with the Department of Linguistics to create a course-integrated program with several undergraduate and all graduate level sections.

As part of the University's general education curriculum, the library collaborates with Composition I instructors of undergraduate level ESL courses. The course-integrated sessions expect that students will have an assignment that requires research following the instruction. The sessions are a distinctive combination of elements, including a discussion comparing home libraries across the world to a U.S. research library environment, an introduction to library databases through a concept mapping exercise that assists students with brainstorming search terms as well as refining search strategies, and evaluating the credibility of various types of information sources.

In developing lesson plans for the graduate level ESL sessions, the Instructional Services Librarian collaborated with the ESL Program Coordinator to examine the curriculum within the context of expanding students' research skills. Specifically, the curriculum of the ESL courses focus on building students' skills in speaking, understanding, reading and writing English. Examples highlight common obstacles that international students face in performing research: an introduction to the conventions of group discussions and formal oral presentations; introduction to paragraph development and organization of academic writing in the U.S.; introduction to the use of rhetorical modes typical of academic writing; introduction to the research paper; review of strategies for effective and critical reading; and special focus on advanced academic writing at the graduate level, including writing such as proposals, research reports, and theses. In response to these struggles, the library developed the following primary learning outcomes for graduate level library instruction at Illinois.

Attendees will:

- Contextualize the expertise of librarians in order to understand how librarians can assist scholars throughout their academic careers;
- Be prompted to ask questions (see below for the Cephalo-

nian Method) about the organization and circulation policies of the library in order to improve understanding of a
research university library system;

- Review citation identification strategies in order to learn
  how to locate a variety of research materials;

- Build on knowledge of subject area(s) and prior searching
  skills in order to conduct successful searches across library
  databases;

- Sign up for a RefWorks account and select from 3 ways to
  import references in order to embark on citation management.

ESL courses present a distinctive learning environment, where diversity permeates the classroom. Students have disparate educational
backgrounds and are at varying stages of their academic careers. They
were raised in different countries, have varying comfort levels with
the English language, have contrasting experiences with libraries, and
are enrolled across disciplines. The instruction classes are supported
by a team of librarians and pre-professional graduate assistants from
the Graduate School of Library and Information Science. Similarly,
the ESL classes are taught by teaching assistants in the Department of
Linguistics. The ESL classroom provides a laboratory for both the ESL
graduate students, library school students and teaching assistants who
are working together to explore the complexities of teaching and learning within a research library.

Active Learning

Haynes (2006) reminds us that, "It is always important for teachers to teach to their students' learning styles but this becomes crucial
when teaching English language learners." In attempting to reach a
variety of learning styles, the Illinois lesson plan includes active learning through the adaptation of the Cephalonian Method (Morgan and
Davies 2004). The Cephalonian Method is a welcoming orientation
strategy that addresses auditory, visual, tactile, kinesthetic, global and
analytical learners (Haynes 2006). Here's how it works: Students are

given color-coded slips of paper that are numbered with general questions about the library. Examples include, "Does the library rent videos?" and "Can we eat in the library?" and "How can I find journal articles?" The librarian prepared a corresponding slide presentation that moves sequentially from question to answer. At the start of the session, the librarian instructs students that when their number is called, they should state their name, their home country, and their field of study and then read the question. The librarian proceeds to answer the question. This icebreaker activity generates conversation in the room and moves naturally into hands-on activities. Questions are updated based on classroom assessment and common interactions with international students. Hensley (2008) reflects that the Cephalonian Method is a "user-centered instruction method where no two sessions are the same, incorporating the element of surprise for both the teacher and the learner."

The Human Boolean (Dempsey 1998) exercise presents international students with an active learning approach to the complexities of Boolean. The instructor divides the classroom by common denominators such as male/female or wearing glasses/not wearing glasses. By asking students to stand up or sit down using the "and" or "or" terminology, students can visualize how to construct an effective Boolean search. In combination with Venn diagrams and database demonstrations, this quick exercise can complement demonstrations of advanced searching strategies. These are only two examples of active learning techniques that promote constructivist learning, an integral component in facilitating a framework of learning for international students.

Workshops

Graduate students, international and American, enter the university with vastly diverse information literacy skills. Since library instruction is not mandated upon admittance or in all courses, students may experience significant gaps in knowledge regarding advanced research skills and information management. One solution is to design a set of open workshops that assist students with critical thinking skills in a number of areas: scholarly communication issues including author rights and open access, plagiarism and academic integrity, citation management, searching for grant funding opportunities, data services, and proficiency around the publication and dissemination of scholarly work (http://www.library.illinois.edu/learn/basics/workshops.html). A workshop on academic integrity encourages students to familiarize themselves with the academic standards of doing research specific to the University of Illinois. Students are introduced to Illinois documents that provide guidelines for academic integrity in teaching, research, service, coursework, research and publication of original student work, as well as information on intellectual property. The session is now part of Illinois' Mechanical and Science Engineering program, one of the largest academic programs teaching international students. Although the library advertises the series of workshops to the entire academic community, attendance is highest among international students.

Online Library Guides for International Students

Online learning opportunities can meet international students at their point of need. As a product of the partnership with the Department of Linguistics, librarians developed several online guides for incoming international students. The guides include basic information about how to use the library including circulation policies, how to access library resources and how to get help from research librarians. Learning modules also include video screencasts with closed-captioning to assist visual learners and to mitigate any language barriers. A glossary of library terms can assist non-native English speakers with the library jargon that inevitably arises when navigating an academic library. The Association of College and Research Library's Multilingual Glossary provides a language table in six languages and a list of definitions of common terms. Consulting with ESL instructors on campus can help clarify terms that may cause unnecessary confusion. The guides at Illinois are available to students as handouts at new student orientation sessions and during course-integrated instruction sessions.

Reference Services

The reference desk can be a place where international students are introduced to a librarian for the first time. By cultivating positive learning experiences and demonstrating the ways in which librarians can support long-term research needs, reference services can play a strong role in the academic life of an international student. When it comes to reference, staff training is imperative in serving an international clientele. Curry and Copeman (2005) remind us of the importance of being approachable, awareness of language barriers, and perhaps most importantly, making sure not to terminate interactions too early. In building reference services, would international students prefer interactions in their native language? Ferrer-Vinent (2010) conducted a study that found most students initially preferred interactions in English with follow-up conversations in their native language if they were not satisfied with the results of the initial transaction. The reference desk can also play the role of the connector, making referrals to the array of campus services that go beyond research support.

Fifth Level—Student Needs

Academic libraries are equipped to assist students with more than basic research needs. By incorporating a civil and sociable environment into the library's daily activities, library personnel can contribute to the diversity of campus life and also help international students feel more at home.

International Film Festivals

Each spring, the Office of International Student Programs coordinates an annual International Education Week. To complement this campus-wide program, the Outreach Librarian for Multicultural Services collaborates with the International Education Week planning committee to sponsor an international film festival. Selected films have included student documentaries, film projects that were created by local faculty, and a variety of films from the library's collections with public performance rights. The partnership with the planning committee presents several key opportunities including recommendations for faculty speakers to introduce films, additional publicity which contributes to higher attendance, and new film suggestions. In selecting for the series, the librarian ensures that each film affirms the library's commitment to encourage attendees to think critically about cultural issues and how those issues translate into daily life. The annual film festival also enables campus community members to come together and discuss each film through facilitated discussions.

Multicultural Library Exhibits

In an effort to generate an environment of inclusion as well as research, the library produces monthly exhibits to promote collections, services, films, and community resources on a defined diverse topic. The exhibits are designed to encourage dialog about different cultures. For instance, each summer the Champaign-Urbana community hosts a food festival, highlighting locally owned restaurants. Festivals present libraries with an ideal opportunity to showcase the community's resources such as international and ethnic restaurants as well as the library's international cookbook collections. Other opportunities include international events such as the Olympics and the World Cup Soccer tournament, which can connect students to the library's collections on current events. Exhibit space also provides additional opportunities to collaborate with on-campus partners to expose their programs and services. For example, the Women's Resource Center and the Native American House collaborated with the library to create exhibits related to violence against women and prejudice against Native American groups. The purpose of exhibits is to encourage students, faculty and staff to engage with the library's dynamic resources and to think critically about current issues and global events.

Resource Allocation

Subject specialists at the University of Illinois are responsible for a collections budget of approximately half a million dollars that is set aside exclusively to support research in area studies and international languages. Additionally, the Outreach Librarian for Multicultural Services oversees a smaller budget to purchase requested items for the offices and student services programs. As many of the area studies specialists select monographs, serials, and online resources, much of the multicultural fund is reserved for acquiring international documentaries and media. Collection development requests, although traditionally reserved for faculty and academic departments, may also be extended to student affairs partners.

Multicultural Resources Portal

The library can play an active role in highlighting activities across campus. Although many universities and libraries offer an array of diverse resources to their constituents, not enough libraries market their services and resources. For instance, Young (2006) conducted a study of thirteen libraries, revealing that only two libraries had a top level link for 'diversity' on their website. As students question what their universities are doing to support diversity initiatives, it is important to communicate what campus programs, services and resources are available and how to gain new information in an easily accessible manner. In 2006, it was apparent that the University of Illinois offered a wide range of diversity and international programs and services for faculty, staff and students; however, the University did not initially host a single clearinghouse to promote diversity programs and initiatives. The library compiled a bibliography of the diverse programs, initiatives, resources, and services that was transformed into a comprehensive web resource for students, faculty, staff and community members. Although the University has since developed a campus-wide portal for diversity and inclusion initiatives, the library's portal also serves as a central place to search for library resources on multicultural, international, multilingual information and library outreach programs.

Sixth Level—Assessment

Assessment is an essential piece for an outreach program in order to meet the needs of an ever-changing international student population.

Instructional Assessment

Library instruction rarely lends itself to comprehensive assessment techniques, hence the decision to use the One Minute Paper Assessment (Angelo & Cross 1993) for Illinois ESL course-integrated instruction. As asserted by Conteh-Morgan (2002), "A more effective technique for ESL learners would be to implement classroom assessment strategies that can provide ongoing and immediate feedback." The One Minute Paper allows instructors to gauge generalized, formative feedback from students. Recent questions include "What is one thing you would still like to know about the library?" and "Was there anything about today's session that confused you?" and "What is the most significant or meaningful thing you have learned during the session?" The questions are changed from semester to semester and the responses help to inform the planning process for following semesters.

Given that responses received from the One Minute paper technique can be off-topic or contain incomplete thoughts, an assessment plan was designed to ask and examine identical questions in each student's first language. Our hypothesis was that more robust feedback would be received if students were allowed to respond in their native language. The librarian worked with ESL teaching assistants to gather the native languages of the students in each class and hired translators to translate the questions and students' answers. A parallel instruction session was used as the control and the assessment was issued in English. Surprisingly, the results did not validate the hypothesis. On average, we received the same number of incomplete responses and superficial feedback from the assessments as conducted in native languages as for the assessments completed in English. Although classroom assessment in native languages may not be necessary, it is still valuable to conduct regular assessment to consistently improve the changing classroom experience.

Conclusion

The most important partners the library has in serving an international student population are the students. A holistic multicultural outreach program can address specific learning needs of international students and can also foster an open conversation regarding diversity among students, faculty and staff. The relationship is mutually beneficial. This chapter proposes elements of developing an outreach and instruction program geared toward reaching international students and that is intertwined by staff training and partnerships. Additional ideas for programming and initiatives include:

- Hosting consulting firms outside the academic environment to offer training programs on cultures around the world;
- Working with university training to develop communication skills with specific groups of international students;
- Conducting institution specific focus groups to examine perceived international student library needs;
- Adapting instructional technology in the classroom that is appropriate for a wide variety of learning styles;
- Developing a peer tutoring service that pairs experienced students of similar cultural backgrounds with new students in order to develop research skills;
- Creating a variety of multilingual resources for top represented languages;
- Networking with campus faculty to explore research areas that enhance library offerings;
- Taking workshops on topics developed for international students into campus departments.

Success resides in a commitment to growth, a willingness to adapt to change and a cohesive communication strategy. The demographics of international student populations will change over time and we have to be willing to embrace the opportunity to consistently reexamine how the library's mission aligns with global perspectives.

Acknowledgments

The authors wish to acknowledge the Research and Publication Committee of the University of Illinois at Urbana-Champaign Library, which provided support for the completion of the research project on assessment in native languages. We would also like to thank Susan Avery, Instructional Services Librarian and Kelsey Keyes, Graduate Assistant at Illinois and all of our student affairs partners for their generous support.

References

Angelo, Thomas A. and K. Patricia Cross. 1993. Classroom assessment techniques: a handbook for college teachers. San Francisco: Jossey-Bass Publishers.

American Library Association. 2006. Multilingual Glossary. <http://www.ala.org/ala/mgrps/divs/acrl/about/sections/is/projpubs/multilingual.cfm> (Accessed January 30, 2011). Document ID: 208712.

Badke, William. 2002. International students: information literacy or academic literacy? *Academic Exchange Quarterly* 6 (4): 60–65.

Baron, Sara and Strout-Dapaz, Alexia. 2001. Communicating with and empowering international students with a library skills set. *Reference Services Review* 29 (4): 314–26.

Conteh-Morgan, Miriam. 2002. Connecting the dots: Limited English proficiency, second language learning theories, and information literacy instruction. *Journal of Academic Librarianship* 28 (4): 191–196.

Conteh-Morgan, Miriam. 2003. Journey with new maps: Adjusting mental models and rethinking instruction to language minority students. *ACRL 11th National Conference:* 1–10.

Curry, Ann and Deborah Copeman. 2005. Reference service to international students: A field stimulation research study. *Journal of Academic Librarianship* 31 (5): 409–20.

Dempsey, Paula and Beth Mark. 1998. Human Boolean exercise. In *Designs for Active Learning: A Sourcebook of Classroom Strategies for Information Education*, eds. Gail Gradowski, Loanne Snavely and Paula Dempsey, 117–118. Chicago: The Association.

Ferrer-Vinent, Ignacio J. 2010. For English, Press 1: International students' language preference at the reference desk. *The Reference Librarian* 51 (3): 189–201.

Goudy, Frank W. and Eugene Moushey. 1984. Library instruction and foreign students: A Survey of opinions and practices among selected libraries. *The Reference Librarian* 10: 215–226.

Haynes, Judie. 2006. *Teach to students' learning styles.* Retrieved on April 2, 2008, from everythingESL.net. <http://www.everythingesl.net/inservices/learning-style.php> (Accessed January 15, 2011).

Helms, Cynthia Mae. 1995. Reaching out to the international students through bibliographic instruction. *The Reference Librarian* (51–52): 295–307.

Hensley, Merinda Kaye. 2008. When the world grows smaller: Renewing instruction methods for international students. In *Proceedings of the 36th annual LOEX conference*, edited by Brad Sietz. Ann Arbor, Mich.: University Library, Eastern Michigan University by Pierian Press: 25–28.

Institute of International Education. 2010. *Open doors 2010: report on international educational exchange*. New York, NY. <http://www.iie.org/en/Research-and-Publications/Open-Doors/Data/International-Students/Leading-Places-of-Origin/2008-10> (Accessed January 20, 2011).

Hendricks, Yoshi. 1991. The Japanese as library patrons. *College & Research Libraries News* 52 (4): 221–225.

Jiao, Qun G., and Anthony John Onwuegbuzie. 2001. Sources of library anxiety among international students. *Urban Library Journal* 11 (1): 16–26.

Lewis, Margaret. 1969. Library orientation for Asian students. *College and Research Libraries* 30 (3): 267–272.

Liestman, Daniel. 1992. Implementing library instruction for international students. *PNLA Quarterly* 56 (2): 11–14.

Love, Emily and Margaret B. Edwards. 2009. Forging inroads between libraries and academic, multicultural and student services. *The Reference Librarian* 37 (1): 20–29.

Natowitz, Allen. 1995. International students in U.S. academic libraries: Recent concerns and trends. *Research Strategies* 13 (1): 4–16.

Moeckel, Nancy and Jenny Presnell. 1995. Recognizing, understanding, and responding: A program model of library instruction services for international students. *The Reference Librarian* 24 (51): 309–325.

Morgan, Nigel and Linda Davies. 2004. Innovative library induction: Introducing the "Cephalonian Method." *Sconul Focus* 32 (Summer/Autumn): 4–8.

Shiflet, Coryn Lee. 2008. *They asked for students, but instead came people with families: A study of higher education migrants in the United States From Brazil, India and China* (MA diss., University of Illinois at Urbana-Champaign, 2008).

University of Illinois. 2010. Facts 2009–2010: Illinois By The Numbers. <http://illinois.edu/about/overview/facts/facts.html> (Accessed January 20, 2011).

University of Illinois. 2009. University of Illinois 2009 Student Data Book. <http://www.pb.uillinois.edu/Documents/databook/Fall2009DBPFinal.pdf> (Accessed January 20, 2011).

Wayman, Sally. 1984. The international student in the academic library. *Journal of Academic Librarianship* 9 (6): 336–341.

Young, Courtney. 2006. Collection development and diversity on CIC academic library web sites. *Journal of Academic Librarianship* 32 (4): 370–376

Chapter 8

Connecting to International Students in Their Languages: Innovative Bilingual Library Instruction in Academic Libraries

Eileen K. Bosch and Valeria E. Molteni

Higher Education in the United States attracts students from all over the world. There is a reasonable amount of literature regarding library instruction to international students; however, there is not much on instruction in students' native languages. This case study was done by two librarians at California State University (Dominguez Hills and Long Beach) where elements of library instruction were offered in Spanish for students taking classes in the Department of Romance Languages. In addition, it will highlight best practices found in the library literature regarding library instruction in students' native languages. The chapter will also discuss the challenges for improving the literacy skills of students studying foreign languages and establishing connections with international students by providing library instruction based on their cultural heritage and languages.

Introduction

It is widely observed in the professional literature, that international students find adjusting to a new country and academic culture challenging. They may experience high levels of stress and isolation during their first year attending college in the United States. Since academic libraries in the United States play an important role in supporting student learning on campus, it is vital that libraries develop and promote multilingual library programs for international students. In an effort to maximize the academic success of these students, several studies have discussed the importance of providing multilingual library instruction (Chakraborty and Tunnon 2000; Jackson 2005; Liestman and Wu 1990; Liu and Winn 2009; Puente, Gray, and Agnew 2009; Spanfelner 1991). In many cases, librarians or library staff may speak more than one language and come from a variety of multicultural, educational, and linguistic backgrounds. It would make sense for academic libraries to utilize librarians' skills, high level of professionalism, and service orientation to provide services, such as library orientations, workshops, subject guides, and tutorials in multiple languages to connect with international students.

This chapter will show how multilingual models in academic libraries can promote information literacy skills and outreach efforts to international students. It will also include a Spanish bilingual model used at California State University, Long Beach (CSULB) and California State University, Dominguez Hills (CSUDH) by two academic librarians who employed their fluency in Spanish as a strategy to connect with students, provide support, and enhance the process of learning in a bilingual library instruction environment. This case study will show that academic librarians can develop unique library services by taking advantage of their skills and personal talents (languages, life experiences, and educational and professional backgrounds) and use them to support student learning experiences.

The librarians developed a conceptual framework for incorporating trans-cultural aspects in library instruction for Spanish-speaking students taking courses in the Spanish Department on both campuses. The goal of this model was to improve students' sense of inclusion and academic persistence. The framework of this model addresses the following elements:

- Bilingualism as a cultural value
- Capacity to find analogies among different Spanish dialects
- Flexibility to modify teaching styles depending on the

students' abilities i.e., dialects, learning styles, information literacy skills, prior learning environment

- Fluency and ability to code-switch languages (switch between a primary and secondary language discourse)
- Openness towards and awareness of cultural differences, particularly language accents
- Ability to transfer information literacy skills in their native languages (in this case, Spanish) to English

The Institutions:

California State University, Long Beach (CSULB) and California State University, Dominguez Hills (CSUDH) are part of the largest, most diverse, and most affordable university systems in the United States. Currently, the California State University System (CSU) has 23 campuses across the state of California. Both campuses are located in the greater Los Angeles area. With a total number of 37,891 students, CSULB is the largest campus in the CSU system and the second largest university in the state. The campus is located in the city of Long Beach and is about thirty miles south of downtown Los Angeles. CSUDH is known as one of the most diverse campuses on the West coast with 12,851 students. It is located in the city of Carson and is about eighteen miles south of downtown Los Angeles. According to the last U.S. Census, approximately 39.9% of the Long Beach population is Latino and Latinos represent approximately 47.1% of the Los Angeles County population (U.S. Census Bureau, 2005–2007 American Community Survey). Currently, both institutions are nationally recognized as Hispanic Serving Institutions (HSI) with 25% or more Latino students.

The Initiative

Building a Case for Spanish Library Instruction for Spanish-speaking Students

One of the major challenges that academic librarians face in teaching international students is finding effective instructional strategies that will address differences in communication, educational experience, and culture. This section will describe how two librarians employed their cultural heritage and fluency in their native language to market unique library instruction in Spanish to teaching faculty in the departments of Romance, German, Russian Languages and Literatures (RGRLL) at CSULB and Modern Languages at CSUDH.

Librarians at CSULB and CSUDH noticed that many students enrolled in Spanish language courses had little in the way of information literacy skills and knowledge of library services. Additionally, it was noted that many students transferred from community colleges and were therefore unfamiliar with the library on their CSU campus. Thus, the authors decided to develop a library instruction model in Spanish. This would address the needs of students by using the authors' South American cultural heritage (Argentina and Peru) and fluency in the Spanish language.

According to a report published by the Modern Language Association, Spanish is the most studied language on college campuses in the United States (Furman, Goldberg, and Lusin 2009). In our experience, many of the students in Spanish language courses at CSULB and CSUDH transfer to the universities from a community college and are unaware of library resources that are available to them, an experience similar to that of the international students.

In an attempt to address the needs of these students, librarians and teaching faculty on both campuses collaborated to develop library instruction sessions that would offer students the required information literacy skills in order to succeed in their courses. Christine Black, Sarah Crest, and Mary Volland (2001) created a librarian-faculty collaboration model (see Figure 8.1) and noted that, "Close collaboration between librarians and faculty during instruction sessions yields a solid learning environment in which subject content blends with the required research and evaluation skills" (222). The authors used this to create an environment that would foster collaboration between teaching faculty and librarians for information literacy instruction. These librarian-faculty bonds can be formed through both formal and informal meetings and communication. Following this model, librarians and faculty began designing and applying the most successful instructional pedagogies and integrating information literacy skills into the curriculum.

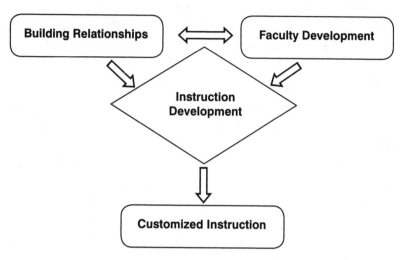

Figure 8.1: Librarian/Faculty Collaboration Model (Black, Crest, and Volland 2001)]

In the fall of 2007, when librarians first presented this unique idea of library instruction in Spanish, faculty members on both campuses were surprised to find that their departments had a librarian who could "teach" and that library instruction could be tailored to the language abilities of their students. Most of the students in these courses were international students or community college transfer students and unaware of library resources. Thus, faculty members were very supportive and enthusiastic about having library instruction sessions in Spanish to better reach their students.

Faculty acknowledged the fact that instruction librarians, who were native Spanish speakers, offered a valuable learning opportunity for students. They decided that during the library instruction session, faculty would introduce librarians as co-instructors, making it clear to students that librarians were part of the academic experience. In addition, the teaching faculty wanted to emphasize to students the importance of listening to another person speak academic Spanish outside of the regular classroom. This presented librarians with an opportunity to speak about their cultural heritage while creating a friendly and warm ambiance that would allow students to feel comfortable when speaking academic Spanish with a stranger.

A Model for Spanish Library Instruction

Librarians approached Spanish language teaching faculty with a plan to offer library instruction in Spanish that addressed the needs of their Spanish-speaking students in upper division courses. At the beginning of each semester, initial contact was made with faculty members. These meetings were done in person, over the phone, or via e-mail. Then, as a follow up to that initial contact, a formal meeting was established where the librarians met with the instructors and discussed the content for the sessions. Here, the librarians paid careful attention to the Spanish course instructor's insight and opinions regarding the information literacy learning outcomes they wanted from the library sessions (see Appendix A). For the most part, the library component was a one-shot instruction session that averaged a total of 90 minutes. Once a lesson plan was outlined, the librarians shared a final instructional plan with the faculty member. This instructional plan contained all the learning elements, tools, and exercises to be used in the session.

Library instruction sessions included: a review of library services, a hands-on activity on searching library databases (when possible), and an overview of the research process. The entire library instruction session was conducted in the Spanish language, and at the end of the class, an evaluation form in Spanish was offered to all students (see Appendix B). The evaluation form was anonymous in order to provide students a non-intimidating way to participate in the assessment. Although not expressed in their formal evaluations, students shared their appreciation of the instruction in Spanish at the end of the class sessions and in subsequent visits to the library.

Conducting the Session

As Miriam Conteh-Morgan (2001) describes, when working with ESL students it is very important to consider five factors in language acquisition: social context, learner characteristics, learning conditions, learning process, and learning outcomes. Conteh-Morgan also supports Cynthia Mae Helms' (1995) vision of an ideal learning environment as one that should have a "small student-teacher ratio, coupled with the teacher's enthusiasm, patience, warm reception, and personalized acceptance and concern for each student" (305). With this in mind, librarians provided a unique "cultural" library instruction experience to Spanish-speaking students.

Librarians created a theme-based "South American" classroom-learning environment where Spanish-speaking students could make cultural connections with librarians, develop a positive perception towards the library, and increase their information literacy skills. To prepare for the class, it was very important that librarians change their body language and incorporate their Latin cultural characteristics. As students entered the classroom, librarians greeted them with a welcoming smile, offered a handshake or a hug, and made students feel "at home." The tone of voice used by librarians was very informal, enthusiastic, and passionate. Librarians emphasized the use of gestures when speaking. Hence, the body language utilized by the librarians addressed the close distance and gesticulation between speakers that is common in Latin cultures.

It was very important to create the feeling that students were coming to a friend's home. Even though these might appear to be minor details, they are key elements in helping to reduce library anxiety and improve learning conditions. Faculty indicated to librarians, anecdotally, that their students showed an instant connection to the librarians' cultural approach.

After students entered the classroom and found their places, the librarians started the lecture with an icebreaker activity by reading a text or poem in Spanish. This gave students the opportunity to listen to the librarians in their native language and subsequently reduce any language barriers or learning anxiety. Both librarians then offered a brief introduction, shared their cultural heritage, and discussed the origin of their Spanish. By sharing their cultural values, librarians were able to establish a friendly and welcoming atmosphere where students could feel relaxed and at ease during the library instruction.

Once the rapport was established, the librarians began to talk about the learning outcomes (see Appendix A) for the library session. First, librarians introduced students to library services such as creating library accounts, borrowing and renewing books, and requesting materials through various interlibrary loan systems, such as ILLIAD (an interlibrary loan and document delivery service) or LINK+ (a cooperative system between 45 academic and public libraries in California and Nevada). The librarians were also continuously engaging students and encouraging them to participate by actively asking questions about the similarities and differences of library services with those in their home countries. This allowed students to speak in their native language while learning information research skills from the librarians. Librarians also taught students how to access research databases from on and off-campus. For most of the sessions, librarians had access to a room with computers where they could integrate a hands-on activity about how to search the different research databases. The hands-on activity prompted students to ask questions in Spanish about navigating the different research databases. Finally, being aware of the students' cultural origins, librarians could incorporate a discussion of the similarities and differences of library services with those they were familiar with from their own countries.

Delivering library instruction in Spanish provided some challenges. The library terminology differed from country to country. For instance, in Spain, the Spanish word for computer is "ordenador" whereas in Argentina and Peru the same term is known as "computadora." In addition, Spanish language courses included a mixture of students for whom English or Spanish was not their first language, as well as native speakers from Spanish-speaking countries. Therefore, librarians needed to be aware of the different language levels of the students in class. To address this, librarians informally assessed the language abilities of the students by starting their library instruction speaking at a slower pace than fluent speakers. Once the librarians were able to identify the language proficiency of the students, they were able to continue their instruction at their native speakers' pace. This strategy helped students get used to the regional accents of both librarians (Argentinean and Peruvian). In addition, it offered a chance for shy students to ask questions in English and then in Spanish, if necessary. The ability to code-switch was tremendously welcomed by students, as they grew more comfortable with the librarians.

Both authors believe that bilingualism is an important asset for any individual, and that speaking other languages opens doors to the cultures of others. As a result, the library instruction sessions were planned to create a classroom environment that promoted a culture of inclusiveness in terms of the different language dialects and skills that each of the students brought to the class (regional accents, proficiency levels, and so on). Library instruction in Spanish offered students an opportunity to exchange different perspectives about their cultures and regional accents and increase their awareness of library services. It also offered the possibility to find analogies among different Spanish dialects (mainly from Latin American), and most importantly, it provided the opportunity for students to celebrate differences and feel enthusiastic about learning.

Even though the evaluations from students were positive, it was difficult to formally measure how offering library instruction in Spanish improved student learning. However, some teaching faculty acknowledged the benefits of our model by providing the following comments:

"Her engaging orientations include the use of academic Spanish while interweaving the jargon of library terms, a notable achievement."

"Since upwards of 85% of students who major or minor in languages in our department are indeed Latinos, this is a key factor in her successful outreach to students…"

As a result of the positive comments provided by teaching faculty, other teaching faculty in the Spanish department have requested library sessions for their courses. At CSULB, faculty teaching other languages such as French, German, and Italian requested the same instructional model, even if the librarian was not fluent in those languages. In sessions where the librarian was not fluent in the course language, the same lesson plan was used, but student volunteers read the poems in the opening session, and students and faculty were encouraged to participate in a larger portion of the instruction. For instance, when teaching students in German classes how to conduct searches in the research databases, the librarian would ask for volunteers to read search results out loud.

To illustrate the flow of the Spanish library instruction, librarians developed a conceptual framework (see Figure 8.2) to visualize how the new instructional model helped improve the information literacy skills of Spanish-speaking students enrolled in Spanish language courses at both institutions. Some of the elements addressed in the framework included:

- Bilingualism as a cultural value
- Capacity to find analogies among the different Spanish dialects
- Flexibility to modify teaching styles depending on the students' abilities i.e., dialects, learning styles, information literacy skills, prior learning environment
- Fluency and ability to code-switch languages
- Openness and awareness towards cultural differences, specifically language accents

Conclusion

The case study described in this chapter was developed with the idea that using the librarians' knowledge and fluency in the students' native language would reduce language barriers to increase the level of research skills. It was also developed to create a culture of inclusiveness where students had the opportunity to validate their cultural identities

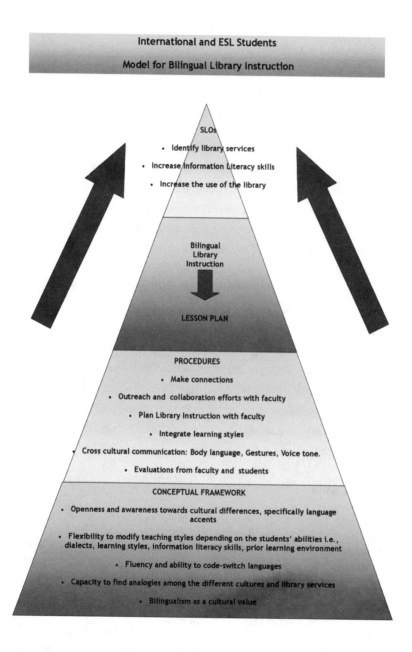

Figure 8.2: Model for Bilingual Library Instruction

and foster positive feelings towards the library as a place for learning. As observed through anecdotal data, students and faculty at CSULB and CSUDH appreciated having Spanish-speaking librarians to help them with their research. Students also indicated that the librarians' approachable styles allowed them to speak and practice their Spanish without the fear of making mistakes in a classroom setting. Moreover, the intent of promoting library instruction in Spanish was to expand the discussion about inserting elements of cross-cultural communication styles when teaching students from different cultures. That is, providing a sense of connectedness between the students, instructors, and librarians. However, further research needs to be conducted to assess the effectiveness of this modelVarious authors recommend the use of bilingual instruction for international students in academic libraries (see Further Readings). Library instruction in the students' native languages has many benefits for international students. It enhances student-library connections, promotes a better understanding of library services in American institutions, augments information literacy skills, and reduces library anxiety. Finally, as this case study has shown, academic librarians can develop unique library services by taking advantages of their skills or personal talents (languages, life experiences, educational and professional backgrounds) and using them to support the learning experiences of the students.

References

Black, Christine, Sarah Crest, and Mary Volland. 2001. "Building a Successful Information Literacy Infrastructure on the Foundation of Librarian-Faculty Collaboration." *Research Strategies* 18 (3): 215–225.

Chakraborty, Mou and Johanna Tunnon. 2000. "Taking the distance out of library services offered to international graduate students: Considerations, challenges, and concerns." *Journal of Library Administration* 37 (1/2): 163–176.

Conteh-Morgan, Miriam. 2001. "Connecting the Dots: Limited English Proficiency, Second Language Learning Theories, and Information Literacy Instruction." *The Journal of Academic Librarianship* 28 (4): 191–6.

Furman, Nelly, David Goldberg, and Natalia Lusin. 2009. "Enrollments in Languages Other Than English in United States Institutions of Higher Education: Fall 2009." Modern Languages of America. Accessed January 17, 2010. http://www.mla.org/pdf/2009_enrollment_survey.pdf.

Helms, Cynthia Mae. (1995). "Reaching out to the International Students through Bibliographic Instruction." *The Reference Librarian* 50/51: 295–307.

Institute of International Education. 2009. *Open Doors 2009 International Students in the United States Report.* Accessed December 18, 2010. http://www.iie.org/en/Who-We-Are/News-and-Events/Press-Center/Press-Releases/2009/2009-11-16-Open-Doors-2009-International-Students-in-the-US.

Jackson, Pamela A. 2005. "Incoming international students and the library: A survey." *Reference Services Review* 33 (2): 197–209.

Liestman, Daniel and Connie Wu. 1990. "Library orientation for international students in their native language." *Research Strategies* 8 (Fall): 191–6.

Liu, Guoying and Danielle Winn. 2009. "Chinese graduate students and the Canadian academic library: A user study at the University of Windsor." *The Journal of Academic Librarianship* 35 (6): 565–73.

Puente, Mark A., LaVerne V. Gray, and Shantel Agnew. 2009. "The expanding library wall: Outreach to the University of Tennessee's multicultural/international student population." *Reference Services Review* 37 (1): 30– 43.

Spanfelner, Deborah L. 1991. "Teaching library skills to international students." *Community & Junior College Libraries* 7 (2): 69–76.

U.S. Census Bureau (2005–2007). "American Community Survey." Accessed March 19, 2011. http://www.census.gov/acs/www/.

Further Readings

Chau, May Ying. 2002/2003. "Helping Hands: Serving and Engaging International Students." *Reference Librarian* 38 (79/80): 383–93.

Downing, Arthur and Leo Robert Klein. 2001. "A Multilingual Virtual Tour for International Students: The Web-Based Library at Baruch College Opens Doors." *College & Research Libraries News* 62 (5): 500–2.

Lo, Mei Ling, Li Sun, Ryan Woman, Connie Wu, and Tao Yang. 2009. "Celebrating Diversity, Welcoming the World: Developing a Chinese Webpage at Rutgers University Libraries." *CALA Occasional Paper Series* 5 (July 2009): 1–11. Accessed November 30, 2010. http://www.cala-web.org/node/293.

Lopez, Manuel D. 1983. "Chinese Spoken Here: Foreign language library orientation tours." *College and Research Libraries News* 44: 265–269.

McClure, Jennifer and Mangala Krishnamurthy. 2007. "Translating the Libraries: A Multilingual Information Page for International Students." *The Southeastern Librarian* 55 (1): 26–31.

Wu, Connie. 1988. "American library terminology—a guide for international students." *Report No: ED 308 863* (1988): *Library, Information Science & Technology Abstracts with Full Text*, EBSCOhost. Accessed December 13, 2010.

Yale University. 2010. "Yale University Library." Accessed November 30, 2010. http://www.library.yale.edu/.

Zhuo, Fu, Jenny Emanuel, and Shuqin Jiao. 2007. "International Students and Language Preferences in Library Database Use." *Technical Services Quarterly* 24 (4): 1–13.

Appendix A – Student Learning Outcomes

List of Student Learning Outcomes:

- Students will be able to navigate the Library's website.
- Students will be able to conduct searches using Online Catalog.
- Students will identify different interlibrary loan services.
- Students will become familiar with Library terminology.
- Students will know the name and contact information for their subject librarian.
- Students will be able to explain the functions of Boolean operators.
- Students will learn the difference between primary vs. secondary resources.
- Students will be able to differentiate between a peer-reviewed journal and other types of articles.
- Students will identify two scholarly journal articles using subject-specific databases.

Appendix B – Spanish Evaluation Form

Nombre del curso: _____

Fecha: _____

Evaluación de la clase de instrucción bibliográfica

1. El instructor presentó el material en forma clara y comprensible:
   - O Totalmente de acuerdo
   - O De acuerdo
   - O En desacuerdo
   - O Totalmente en desacuerdo

2. La clase estuvo bien organizada y fluida
   - O Totalmente de acuerdo
   - O De acuerdo
   - O En desacuerdo
   - O Totalmente en desacuerdo

3. El instructor/a mostró interés y entusiasmo
   - O Totalmente de acuerdo
   - O De acuerdo
   - O En desacuerdo
   - O Totalmente en desacuerdo

4. El material impreso entregado es útil
   - O Totalmente de acuerdo
   - O De acuerdo
   - O En desacuerdo
   - O Totalmente en desacuerdo

5. Luego de la clase de instrucción bibliográfica, me siento más cómodo en emplear la biblioteca para mi investigación
   - O Totalmente de acuerdo

O De acuerdo
O En desacuerdo
O Totalmente en desacuerdo

6. Evalúe en forma global la clase de instrucción bibliográfica
O Sobresaliente
O Excelente
O Bueno
O Suficiente
O Pobre

7. ¿Cómo puede ser mejorada esta clase?

8. Por favor incluya aquí comentarios adicionales

Evaluation form created by Valeria E. Molteni

Chapter 9

Addressing Academic Integrity: Perspectives From Virginia Commonwealth University in Qatar

Nancy Fawley

Understanding the cultural aspects that affect a student's ability to appropriately use resources is important in developing outreach and instruction in multicultural settings. Differences in educational philosophies, students' previous scholastic training and cultural differences in individual motivation are all factors that may affect a freshman's ability to understand an American university's idea of academic integrity and can inadvertently cause problems where independent work and critical thinking are required. At Virginia Commonwealth University in Qatar (VCUQatar), a branch campus of the American university in the Middle East, a special class on academic integrity and ethical behavior was integrated into the freshman introduction to the university course. The class focused on fictional case studies that addressed each of the six violations of the university's honor code in situations that reflected the school's diverse student body.

Introduction

In an attempt to address cultural differences that affect a student's understanding of a university's honor code in a branch campus of an American university in the Middle East, a special class was integrated into the freshman introduction to the university course. This class, co-taught by a librarian and a writing center instructor, focused on fictional case studies that addressed each of the six violations of the university's honor code in situations that reflected the school's diverse student body. The aim was to provoke a conversation and encourage the students to think critically about the choices they will make in their academic career and beyond.

The Institution

Virginia Commonwealth University in Qatar (VCUQatar) is a branch campus of Virginia Commonwealth University's School of the Arts in Richmond, Virginia, and was established in 1998 through a partnership between VCU and the Qatar Foundation for Education, Science and Community Development. The mission of the university is to provide a high level of design education for the citizens of Qatar. VCUQatar offers Bachelor of Fine Arts degrees in Communication Arts and Design, Fashion Design and Merchandising, and Interior Design. A Painting and Printmaking program was recently added as well as an M.F.A. program in Interdisciplinary Design. It is a small university with 231 students and 40 teaching faculty, with an average freshman class of approximately 70 students. Fifty-seven percent of the student population is native Qatari. Thirty-three nationalities are represented at the school, but students hail primarily from the surrounding Middle Eastern countries. The language of academic instruction is English and

Figure 9.1: VCUQatar Freshman class of approximately 70 students

most of the students speak English as a second or third language. A TOEFL (Test of English as a Foreign Language) score of at least 550 on the paper-based test is a requirement for admittance and students' scores range from around 500 to over 600 out of a possible 677. As a result, the school has students with a wide range of English language skills, which affect their ability to use the library and to successfully complete the necessary coursework for their degrees.

Education In Qatar

Qatar is a small peninsula approximate in size to the U.S. state of Connecticut and is bordered by Saudi Arabia and the Arabian Gulf. The population of Qatar is 1.7 million people and most reside in the capitol city of Doha (Qatar Statistics Authority 2010). Only about one-fourth of the population is native Qatari; the remainder is made up of expatriate workers, the majority of whom are low-wage laborers from the Indian subcontinent. Before independence in 1971, Qatar was a British protectorate and its main industry was pearl diving. Oil and natural gas have created great wealth and made Qatar one of the fastest growing countries in the world. According to the CIA World Factbook, Qatar boasts the world's second highest per-capita income.

Qatar is committed to nurturing "brains before oil wells" and to moving from a reliance on natural resources to a knowledge-based society (Hanley 2007). To facilitate this shift, the Qatari government has launched ambitious educational reforms at all levels, including the improvement of post-secondary educational opportunities. The Qatar Foundation, a private, non-profit organization founded in 1995 by the current Emir of Qatar, His Highness Sheikh Hamad Bin Khalifa Al-Thani, is primarily responsible for sponsoring these reforms. The purpose of the Qatar Foundation, headed by the Emir's consort, Her Highness Sheikha Mozah Bint Nasser Al-Missned, is to create a network of educational centers devoted to progressive education, research and community development. The organization's flagship project is Education City, a 2500-acre campus situated on the outskirts of Doha that houses, among other knowledge institutions, six branch campuses of American universities: Carnegie-Mellon in Qatar, Georgetown School of Foreign Service in Qatar, Northwestern University in Qatar, Texas A & M in Qatar, VCUQatar and Weill-Cornell Medical College.

The state also has a goal of "Qatarization," an initiative to bring more Qataris into employment in the private sector. Foreigners make up most of the workforce in the private sector industries such as petrol, finance and higher education; the challenge has been to hire qualified and motivated locals for these positions. In order to achieve the state's goal of becoming a knowledge-based society, Qataris must be able to obtain the education and achieve the test scores to be admitted to the elite American universities in their country. As a result, the state has also embarked on an ambitious project to reform the K though 12 curriculum. In 2002, a new ministry, the Supreme Education Council, was established to oversee the independent schools and strengthen the curriculum in English, science and mathematics.

The Education City universities are unique in that they are coed and men and women attend classes together. In Qatar, local customs strictly prohibit any interactions between men and women who are not related or married. The local university, Qatar University, has separate men's and women's schools and separate libraries, as do all the local schools, with the exception of international schools. Furthermore, most local women are not allowed to travel abroad without a father or a brother as chaperone. Thus, the American university branch campuses enable them to get an American university degree without leaving their homes and families. Men are able to go abroad without permission, but there is always the chance they may not want to return home.

Cultural Context

Developing an understanding of the educational system of students' home countries is essential in developing outreach and information literacy instruction. In the Middle East and Asia, many libraries have closed stacks, while some libraries are reserved for scholars to use, not students (Leki 1992, 74). In Qatar, for instance, many local schools do not have a library, and those that do may have a closed-stacks policy where only teachers and library staff can access the collection. Many of the library staff in these schools have a high-school diploma or a bachelor's degree and little formal training in public services and information literacy. As a result they play more of a "keeper of the library" role, discouraging students from touching the collection, rather than engaging and instructing them in the use of the library and its resources. Furthermore, notions of access and service for everyone regardless of their social standing is not always accepted in highly segmented societies such as those in the Persian Gulf (Wand 2010).

English language proficiency, especially the understanding of discipline-specific terms, can be a challenge for English as a Foreign Language (EFL) students and is probably one of the main reasons they plagiarize or unintentionally misuse sources. International students reading and writing in English, as a second language may not feel confident using their own words. Communicating original thoughts involves selecting and organizing words and phrases that may be beyond their level of language development. They may plagiarize simply because they do not have the necessary vocabulary or language skills to complete the assignment.

Cultural differences in educational philosophies are one aspect that relate to the notion of academic integrity that universities stress. In many countries in the Middle East and Asia, teaching is by rote memorization and imitation. The only book used in class is a textbook and students are expected to memorize and repeat it verbatim in an exam. Critical thinking and problem solving are not required or expected. In Hong Kong, another region that historically teaches by rote, students had few opportunities to write essays and were primarily required to take exams, which tested the knowledge of the course book through memorization (Pennycook 1996, 223–224). Memorizing text in one's native language then, does little to prepare a student to think critically.

Furthermore, good students do not challenge their teachers or authorities, but faithfully copy and reproduce them (Sowden 2005). In many cultures memorizing the writing of ancient scholars, or the Quran in Muslim cultures for example, is a way of showing respect and honoring the creator and is an important part of scholarly and religious training. Copying another person's work is also seen as a sign of respect. Conversely, writing one's own thoughts may seem "immodest and presumptuous" (Leki 1992, 71). In Arab societies where there is a deep attachment to their language, (Hamady 1960, 19), students may copy simply because they like the way the words are written. Changing them might imply that the student thinks he could do better.

Attitudes towards private property and ownership differ throughout the world and are another aspect to keep in mind when working with international students. Countries with a tradition of writing develop ideas of intellectual property rights (Leki 1992, 71). In traditionally oral Arab culture, the information comes from wisdom, poetry, and songs and folk stories, not books. In this respect, information is essentially in the public domain. Repeating someone else's words is part of the oral tradition and is a way of passing information from one generation to the next.

Another characteristic of the traditional nomadic Bedouin society is that it is group-oriented; the focus in on the family or tribe, not the individual. The Arab proverb, "one hand alone cannot applaud," expresses this idea of mutual interdependence (Hamady 1960, 28). Cohesion and conformity to the group's codes were necessary for survival in the desert and goals were set based on the improvement of the fate and position of the family (Patai 2002, 83). Personality traits, such as independent thinking, that did not strengthen the group were not encouraged and were punished; independent needs were subordinate as well. This conflicts with the individual, performance-related goals Western culture prizes. Sincerity, loyalty and devotion to the family are character traits that still exist today.

In group-oriented societies there is also pressure to help the weaker members succeed. In this instance, helping a friend or a relative is not considered cheating but a moral obligation (Leki 1992, 72). Working together as a group, even when the assignment is to be done individually, is not considered cheating. Different cultures have different ideas as to what constitutes appropriate collaboration and this creates a conflict in a Western university setting where there are distinct rules as to what is considered acceptable in this situation.

The Initiative

At VCUQatar, freshmen are required to take a one-credit *Introduction to the University* course that introduces new students to the expectations and purposes of a university education and focuses on the skills needed to have a rewarding and successful academic experience. The course is taught by university counselors and combines lectures with visits from guest speakers to introduce students to the resources available to them during their academic career.

A class on academic integrity is included in the course, and the library and writing center collaborated to develop the guest lecture for the class. Violations of academic integrity are a concern to all universities, but for VCUQatar freshmen this might be the first time they have learned that these actions are not acceptable and may result in academic probation, or suspension from school. Plagiarism is the violation that is most well known to the students. The other five violations are cheating, facilitating academic dishonesty, abuse of academic materials, stealing academic materials, and lying related to academic matters.

These violations should be obvious to those who have studied at Western institutions, but might be foreign concepts for those educated in another culture. It was important that the class addressed all the possible violations, but at the same time did it in an engaging and non-threatening manner. The aim was to develop an interactive learning situation that would facilitate discussion on each violation. Six fictional case studies were written, each addressing one violation of the honor code (Appendix A). The aim was to make them interesting, relevant and easy for second language learners to comprehend. The discussion would focus on alternatives and solutions for students who might find themselves in a similar situation. The case studies reflected situations that occur in the region, such as hiring someone to complete assignments or helping a relative with course assignments, and were relevant to a design school. Our fictional characters were given names common to the region and we created avatars that reflected the diversity of our student population.

The case studies were intentionally ambiguous to force the students to think critically about the situation and the potential consequences. Ostensibly, students could make these violations without suffering the consequences, so we also wanted them to think about the ethical implications of making right and wrong decisions regardless of whether or not one gets caught. There are no clear-cut solutions to these situations; they are related to the personal choices one makes. The aim was to help students make the choices that would enable them to have a positive academic experience.

To address this, the class started with a brief, 10-minute lecture on ethics, integrity and values and how these qualities relate to the principles of right and wrong. The lecture linked ethical behavior to the mutual trust between professors and students, and linked integrity to the courage to act with sincerity and honesty. Personal values were also linked to religious beliefs. In Qatar and other countries in the region, there is no separation of church and state. It is understandable that raising the issue of personal religious beliefs in a university course may seem inappropriate to those raised in societies where the two are separated by law. Admittedly, it was risky to discuss this, but the concept resonated with the students and helped them to better understand the complex ideas we were discussing.

We used different approaches to the student participation portion of the class. Initially we talked about each case as a group. The class would debate the morality of the situation, and discuss what might drive a student to do this. This topic would then lead to a conversation of who might also be affected by the actions of the student in the case study. Finally, the class discussed strategies for avoiding similar situations, where one might get help, and alternate choices of actions.

In case study two, for example, two friends are in the same animation class. James, the struggling student, hires a professional to complete his assignments and is suddenly excelling in class. The class might start by discussing the alternative options James could pursue to get help in the class and the course of action his friend, Ahmed, who knows about his cheating, could take. The students also discuss the affect this has on the others in the class who are doing their own work, and how this will affect James as he moves onto more difficult animation courses and eventually a career. The discussions are fluid and not highly planned. The direction the conversations take are dictated by the students comments, although there are always certain points we want to make about each case. The solutions we discuss are related to the roles the library and writing center play in the university, plus the help students can get from their faculty and the university counselors.

More recently, we have experimented with breaking the class up into six groups and assigning each group a case study. They have ten minutes to talk amongst themselves; then share with the class one reason why the scenario is ok and one reason why it is not. Again, the aim is to get students to think critically about the situation and the possible consequences. Both approaches worked equally well, although the students had more difficulty staying on task when they were in groups. As instructors who have taught this class for over three years, we appreciated the opportunity to try a different approach. It keeps us fresh and interested in the instruction as well.

The concepts learned in this class are followed up by four research methods workshops, titled "Work Faster and Get Better Grades," which focus on the plagiarism violation of the honor code. These workshops were a response to complaints from faculty on the quality of writing first-year students produce in their freshmen composition classes. The first workshop addresses plagiarism, but is taught from the point-of-view that most students unintentionally plagiarize, or misuse sources, because of careless or inadequate use of citing and an inability to take adequate notes and paraphrase properly. Instead of dwelling on the problem, each subsequent class focuses on a separate solution: paraphrasing a source, summarizing a source, and directly quoting a source. And, rather than focus on the definitions of these solutions, the students spend much of the workshops writing and practicing these techniques. The logic is that students will learn more by doing, in this case by paraphrasing a paragraph, than by listening to a lecture on how to do it.

Each workshop follows a similar structure; the first 15 minutes is a lecture where the concepts are explained and questions answered. It is helpful when lecturing to a class of EFL students to think back to when you learned a foreign language and remember how difficult it was to understand someone when they spoke quickly. Speaking slowly may seem like obvious advice, but it is easy to forget and even easier to speed up your speech when you are nervous, or enthusiastic, about instruction. Also, choose words carefully and use a simple sentence structure; avoid library specific jargon and opt for more commonly used terms. At the same time, do not simplify the content you are teaching so much that you appear to be condescending. Use active learning techniques rather than a straight lecture format; ask students questions and listen carefully to their answers. This keeps them involved in the class and their learning and helps you to know whether or not the students understand the content.

The rest of the hour the students spend writing, first in groups and then later on their own. Group work was included in the workshop to engage the students in the task and to allow those with weak language skills to benefit from their more proficient peers. After the class reviews the group assignment, students complete another short writing assignment on their own. Both assignments involve paraphrasing a short paragraph and citing it properly. The challenge was finding a suitable paragraph at a reading level that would not discourage and frustrate the students. We also prefer to use design-related topics that are relevant to the curriculum and of interest to the freshmen. We also listed any unusual or difficult words with their meanings and synonyms on the handouts. All individual assignments are reviewed and the first part of the subsequent class is spent addressing any problems the students had completing the assignment and any questions they asked on the feedback form.

Conclusion

In universities with large international student populations, it is important to develop library instruction that addresses the cultural differences that may affect students' abilities to succeed academically. International students come from a variety of different educational systems that may place value on attributes such as memorization and group work that are at odds with critical thinking and independent work expected at their host schools.

At VCUQatar, we have the luxury of working with a small group of students and faculty that allows us to spend more time with outreach and instruction. Small student class sizes also enable us to engage the freshmen in more intimate class discussions and group work. The activities described here address cultural differences, but they also reflect the changing role of librarians, where at many institutions it is it simply not enough to teach bibliographic instruction. Librarians must also work collaboratively with their peers in student services and the writing center to prepare students for a successful academic career.

References

Hamady, Sania. 1960. *Temperament and Character of the Arabs.* New York: Twain.

Hanley, Delinda C. 2007. Qatar's Education City is Building Bridges To a Better Future. *The Washington Report on Middle East Affairs* (August). http://www.wrmea.com/archives/August_2007/0708030.html.

Leki, Ilona. 1992. *Understanding ESL Writers: A Guide for Teachers.* Portsmouth, NH: Boynton/Cook.

Patai, Raphael. 2002. *The Arab Mind.* Long Island City: Hatherleigh Press.

Pennycook, Alastair. 1996. Borrowing Others' Words: Test, Ownership, Memory, and Plagiarism. *TESOL Quarterly* 30 (2): 210–230

Sowden, Colin. 2005. "Plagiarism and the Culture of Multilingual Students in Higher Education Abroad." *ELT Journal* 59 (3): 226–233. Omni File Full Text. WilsonWeb. VCUQ Lib., Doha, Qatar. 28 February 2007 <http://vnweb.hwwilsonweb.com>.

Qatar. *CIA World Factbook.* 2011. https://www.cia.gov/library/publications/the-world-factbook/geos/qa.html.

Qatar Statistics Authority. 2010. http://www.qsa.gov.qa/eng/index.htm.

Wand, Patricia. 2010. *Core Values and Cultural Context: Understanding the Fundamentals. Leaders Look Toward the Future: A Companion Website to Academic Librarianship.* http://www.neal-schuman.com/academic/Wand2010.pdf

Appendix A: Academic Integrity Case Studies

Case One

As Sara was writing her works cited page for an art history paper she realized she forgot to make a note of where she found some of the information she cited. The information was too important to not include it, plus if she deleted it the paper would be too short. Instead, she found a website with similar information and cited that one instead.

Is this OK?

Case Two

Ahmed and James are best friends who are majoring in Graphic Design. Whenever possible, they schedule their courses together, and this semester both are taking a special topics course in animation. Ahmed seems to be especially talented in developing animation: his characters display interesting three-dimensional personalities, and the movements they use convey even more information than their dialogues.

At first James seems to be struggling in this course. His characters seem flat and one-dimensional, although he does have a talent for composing snappy dialogues. By the middle of the semester, James is earning a "C" in the course and is worried about his grade point average, so he hires an animator in Dubai to help him improve his grade by completing the animation projects that he starts.

His professor notices that James's work has suddenly become quite polished and is very suspicious. When he asks James what happened, James just says that he finally "got it" about animation. No one knows about James's help from a professional except Ahmed, and Ahmed will not tell on his best friend.

Is this OK?

Case Three

Said's friend is studying law in the UK. His friend told him that the school is so competitive that students will go to the library and hide books so that their classmates will not be able to find the best information and get the better grade.

Is this OK?

Case Four

Shelly is analyzing a work of art for a paper in her English class. She has composed three pages of the paper based on her careful observations of the formal elements in the painting, such as the artist's use of line, color, and size. She needs two more pages to complete the assignment but just cannot think of anything else to write about the painting.

Imagine Shelly's surprise today when the guest speaker invited to her Survey of World Art class is an authority on the artist who painted the work she is analyzing! The guest speaks to the class about research he is conducting that is bringing new insight to this artist's work, and he discusses several unique brush strokes the artist used to convey depth, shadows, and movement. In addition, Shelly learns about the symbolism of several items that are always included in her artist's works. She realizes that the work of art she has chosen contains these items, and she takes very detailed notes of the talk so she can include all of this new information in her paper.

Is this OK?

Case Five

Aisha was meeting with one of her professors when the Dean stopped by to ask him a quick question. While he was out of his office, she noticed a copy of her class's upcoming exam on his desk. She did not touch the exam but did take an upside-down peak at some of the questions. After all, it was the professor's fault to leave it sitting on his desk.

Is this OK?

Case Six

Fatima's older sister, Haya, has her degree from VCUQatar and took MATH 001 two years ago. Haya understands algebra much better than Fatima and has agreed that Fatima can borrow her extensive notes from the course, including her solutions to the homework problems in the textbook if Fatima promises to study each problem to be sure she understands it before she copies it for her own homework. Haya has offered to explain any of the problems that Fatima does not understand.

This process works well for Fatima until mid-term exams approach. In addition to studying for two difficult tests, Fatima also must complete a complicated design project to hand in the same day her math homework for Unit 4 is to be collected. Fatima promises herself to review the homework problems with Haya after the mid-term and copies them quickly so she can hand them in on time yet still complete her project and study for the two exams.

Is this OK?

Chapter 10

Addressing Deeper Issues of Information Literacy in Graduate International Students: A Korean Student Case Study

William Badke

"It is a grace for me to study Research Strategies at TWU. I haven't learned this way and this subject. Even though this course is hard to me and my understanding of this would be less than other students, I have a privilege to study your subject."
—ACTS Worldview Student

Associated Canadian Theological Schools of Trinity Western University has a division of its M.A. program entitled Worldview Studies in Korean (WS). It is a graduate level offering for Korean professionals seeking to study worldview issues related to their chosen professions. The program demands a high level of critical thinking and a number of research papers. Unfortunately, the institution's required one credit research course became a serious challenge for students in Worldview Studies, resulting in poor grades and limited achievement of the course's goals. In concert with the program director, the librarian has initiated a number of remedial solutions. This paper discusses these initiatives, their successes and their limitations.

Introduction

In 2008, there were over 187,000 international students in Canada, most of these from Asia. The most common country of origin was China, but Korea was a close second, far ahead of other nations, including the United States (Roslyn Kunin & Associates 2009). The following case study looks at a graduate seminary program in which the challenges to provide high quality information literacy instruction to Korean students seemed at first insurmountable until innovative approaches to the problem proved somewhat more successful.

The Institution

Associated Canadian Theological Schools (ACTS) is the Graduate School in Theology of Trinity Western University, a private Christian university near Vancouver, BC, Canada. The programs at ACTS are rigorous in their training of pastors, counselors and lay people at the graduate level. Many courses feature research papers, and the emphasis on student research is supported by a required one-credit informational research course within all of its programs. Rejecting the path of indoctrination, ACTS expects its students to think critically and determine their own answers to life issues.

Within the Master of Arts in Christian Studies there is one division unlike any other at ACTS—Worldview Studies in Korean (WS), that is comprised exclusively of Korean students. With the rapid growth of Christianity in Korea over the past few decades, professionals, many of them with existing master's degrees and even doctorates, have felt the need for a course of study that enables them to integrate their Christian worldview with their professions. These students are scientists, social scientists, business people, schoolteachers, and so on, covering a wide range of professions. Some come from religious studies backgrounds where they serve as pastors or instructors.

What, essentially, is a worldview? It is that complex set of beliefs about the world and one's place or role in it that guides attitudes and conduct in daily life. If I, for example, am a distrustful person who suspects that most people are selfish and that my role is to protect myself from those who may harm me, my worldview will be that of paranoia, resulting in behaviors of isolation and self-preservation. If I believe that the supreme goal of life is to become powerful, my motives and actions will be guided by that worldview. A Christian worldview will rest upon biblically-based theological beliefs and will be characterized by a mixture of concern for ethics and a desire to serve humanity. An example of an ethical consideration might be caring for the earth, while a service consideration might be incorporating patterns of servant leadership into directing a company. The worldview, ultimately, forms an explanation for why people think and act the way they do.

In a country like Korea, where educational systems are heavily influenced by Confucianism, itself a worldview as much as it is a religious philosophy, the idea of practicing a profession without a worldview is simply not entertained. Thus WS was created at ACTS to provide graduate students with an opportunity to engage with worldview issues (often ethical ones) of many kinds, in an atmosphere of critical thinking and exploration. The program is run by a Korean-trained Ph.D. in physics, who has also completed a master's degree in theological studies in the United States. He is strongly supportive of research training for his students.

Over the past few years, it has become increasingly difficult to recruit Korean students who have sufficient ability with English to meet entrance requirements. Since most of the courses are taught in Korean, or in English with Korean interpretation, ACTS, beginning in 2008, agreed to admit students without a specific English requirement. That is, all TOEFL entrance requirements (the normal measure for determining English ability) were waived and English competency was no longer tested as part of student admission to WS. All Korean university graduates do have at least some English competency, based on required English instruction in Korea, and this competency was deemed sufficient to enable them to function within WS.

From its beginning, WS has included the one credit research course, the same course required in all ACTS programs. The Research Strategies course (RES 500—Research Strategies), taught either live or online, involves instruction and assignments that call for formulating research questions and thesis statements, searching catalogs and databases, evaluating information, and constructing a final annotated outline and bibliography or a research paper. Students from the WS program have consistently found the research course very difficult and have tended not to score well in their final grades. After the removal of an English requirement for student admission, students with limited English ability entered the program, and the difficulty level increased. For this author, the challenge of grading increasingly ungrammatical material written in English led him to question the viability of requiring the research course in WS.

Cultural Context

Education within Korea can be characterized as pronouncedly hierarchical. The personal goal at all levels is to be the best student from the best school, and the consequences for failing to achieve this are serious. Early education culminates at the high school level with an onerous university entrance examination for which many students begin preparing as early as kindergarten. Since the universities are ranked hierarchically and the best schools are funded to the highest level by the government, the guiding motivation of students is to score well on the entrance exam so that they may go to the best university possible. The examination score determines the type of university to which the student may apply and thus often the career level to which a graduate may rise.

For pre-university studies, the looming examination essentially dictates that the educational emphasis will rest upon learning content. While creative thinking is encouraged, there is not really time in the student's school life to wander far from the core curriculum. This same emphasis on content as opposed to process continues in undergraduate university studies, where the lecture method predominates and the ability to memorize is seen as a test of intelligence.

Students, even during university undergraduate studies, are given little instruction in writing academic papers and, in fact, write few such papers (Cho 2010). They also find themselves caught in the rather unusual situation of struggling to read Korean language academic books, due to the large number of Chinese characters in them, a holdover from the Hanja writing system. Hanja was traditionally the written Korean language of academics and cultured people. It features the use of a significant number of Chinese characters that stand for Korean words. Korean readers, of course, have to be able to interpret these characters correctly to read Hanja. The other, and much more widely used, writing system is Hangul, which is comprised entirely of Korean characters.

Hanja has largely been abandoned for most written communication in Korea except for that of traditionally oriented academic writers. In its place, the Hangul writing system predominates. Hanja is not required for entrance exams to university, so students often do not learn the Chinese characters well and tend to use Hangul almost exclusively. Faced in university with many academic writings written in Chinese character-based Hanja, many students instead do their reading and writing from English academic sources, though they find this difficult and the results are less than desirable.

The actual amount of reading done by university students in Korea is thus quite limited, and this creates problems when they begin studying in the West. One participant in Cho's study of Korean scholars studying in the United States said this: "I am so mad that they [my teachers in Korea] never taught me how to read and write. I've come to think that reading and writing should be taught at high school. Not just in English. Even in Korean…. I thought that I had read a lot but the amount of my reading is not comparable to that of other American students" (Cho 2010, 87).

A great deal of the educational philosophy of Korea, as in a number of other Asian cultures, is based upon Confucianism. While the Korean education system has declared a separation from this guiding worldview, it is still pervasive. Confucianism, a philosophy more than a religion, emphasizes doing what is right over doing what is expedient, honoring parents and others in authority, working hard, and maintaining general good order in society. Lee (2001) argues: "The ultimate goal of Confucian ethical values is to build personal and sociopolitical order in collectivist society." While these traits can be seen as helpful to successful education, they tend to work better in a controlled environment in which students are learners and teachers are revered and not challenged. That is the case in Korea, where students honor their teachers who, in turn, deal with their students like benevolent, but very much in-control parents. Free discussion of academic topics is relatively rare, and most education is unidirectional, from teacher to student.

A further cultural factor that influences Korean education is the role of the traditional society in Korean life. Traditional societies are based upon the guiding principle that the longstanding knowledge base of the group is the means of its survival. Such societies depend upon crucial knowledge, passed from generation to generation, to enable crops to flourish, medical healing to succeed, and deities to be appeased. Knowledge in such societies has intrinsic value. Children learn it, whether or not they see its relevance, simply because it must be learned. Such societies tend not to encourage the unlearned to question or challenge or, indeed, to add to the knowledge base, because knowledge is too precious to be modified by any but the most recognized experts. In such a context, education tends to be characterized more by the imparting of knowledge than by experimentation within an environment of critical thinking (Badke 2002). Both the traditional society ethos and Confucianism find congruence in this emphasis.

Korea, of course, has now become highly advanced industrially, and is one of the most developed nations in the world when it comes to the use of technology. This has created inevitable clashes with the existing educational philosophy as more Western concepts of free inquiry and student self-learning have begun to have an effect. Yet, educational structures being inherently slow to change, there is little evidence that Korean students are experiencing dramatic revision in the ways in which they are taught. Kwon & Danaher (2001) summarized the student- professor relationship as follows: "This respect and loyalty are evident in the custom of bowing slightly in the presence of the lecturer, using formal titles, speaking only when asked to do so and avoiding publicly challenging the lecturer's knowledge or authority" (115).

Thus we have Korean students, whether at undergraduate or even graduate levels, who have relatively little experience with Western approaches to inquiry and research. While they are skilled at knowledge assimilation, few of them have written extensive critical research essays or even experienced the sort of give and take found in the standard Western university classroom. Though the industrial and technological advances in Korean life over the past few decades have introduced Western ways, the education system has not changed significantly.

Many of the students who enter ACTS Worldview Studies have graduated from various Korean public universities; some having achieved master's degrees and even doctorates. Others have studied at seminaries where most have received master's degrees. All of these students are intelligent and highly motivated, having had positive experiences with higher education in the past. Yet universally, they find the one-credit ACTS Research Strategies course to be exceedingly challenging, and their grades tend to be discouraging, indicating low levels of information literacy attainment as we in the West have defined it. At first I believed that their intense struggles with the English language were at the heart of their problem, but I came to understand that the more serious challenge was a difference in educational philosophy.

While Korean students are used to a highly personal relationship with a professor, who is more of a father or mother than merely a teacher to them, average North American students have only passing relationships with those who teach them. While North American professors want students who are able to think for themselves, Korean professors closely mentor their students, guiding them into a shared truth that comes from the professor's own worldview. While Korean students do not challenge their professors, North American students do this regularly. While research in North America is intended to focus on discovery and problem-solving, the experience of Korean students, up into even the master's level, tends to be that of shaping their inquiries to imitate and even celebrate the views of their teachers.

English ability, admittedly, is a contributing factor in barriers to learning within a North American setting. This is especially true of Koreans, for whom the learning of English seems to be a particularly difficult task, due to the differences in the way each language is structured. An interview with Se-Yeoung Chun, president of Korea Education & Research Information Service included this account: "'Korean people really hate English. It's just a struggle. It's like a demon, you know,' he said with a laugh, as two of his colleagues laughed nervously at his frankness. 'We cannot escape from the demon. We must fight with the demon'" (Young 2010).

The Initiative

When Associated Canadian Theological Schools (ACTS) began in 1987, its curriculum included a one-credit course—Research Strategies—required within all programs. The course itself, at first taught live and, as of 2000, taught in live or online options, stresses development of a bank of strategies for informational research, from initial formulation of research questions or thesis statements through information gathering in a variety of formats (with an emphasis on technological tools) to information evaluation and application to meet the goal of the research project. The course is intensive in the number of assignments required. These are based on real projects, which students are researching in other courses, and the Research Strategies assignments require students to actually carry out research in several stages, documenting their results (Badke 2010a; Badke 2010c). There are no examinations, only a series of hands-on research assignments focused on genuine research projects.

Example of a Research Strategies Course Assignment
FOR BEGINNING OF CLASS 7: (Read Research Strategies, pp. 76-95. Indicate in your assignment that this reading has been done.)

State your research question. Indicate if you have modified it from last week's version.

1. Do an article search using two of the journal databases accessed through the TWU library homepage or one of the terminals in the library. Be sure the databases are relevant to your topic, and indicate what databases you used (full titles of databases, not just "EBSCO" or "ProQuest"). You MUST use subject headings as well as keywords if subject headings are available in your databases and relevant to your searches.

2. Indicate what subject terms or keywords you used in your searches. These will tell me if you used lateral thinking and if you formulated your search too broadly. Keep your searches simple, relevant and few (no more than 3 or 4 search word combinations).

3. List 10 articles from each database that are relevant to your topic—author, article title, title of journal, volume number, date, page numbers. You will be graded on relevance. Some of the articles in each list may be the same or they may be different.

4. Check the availability of each article. Is it available in full text right within the database you are searching? If not, is it available in our library (in another database or another format)? If so, indicate the database or format in which it will be found.

Rubric for an answer achieving full marks:
- Chooses the best two databases for the topic
- Creative use of terminology, including controlled vocabulary if available
- Articles are on target to help in addressing the research question. Indicates availability of all articles

The online version of Research Strategies was created in 2000, initially to meet the needs of students not in WS who were located at a distance from the seminary. With the growth of electronic search tools, it was possible for our students to "use" the library to a large extent without actually visiting the physical library. Very quickly, however, the online version became a favorite even for locally based students due to the time flexibility it offered to students, who were not locked into a course timetable, though they still had due dates. It was easy to create online modules out of the assignment sets from the in-person course without changing, to any great degree, the nature of the assignments. The online version did, however, offer much more potential to provide animated tutorials and links to needed information on the Internet.

The Worldview Studies in Korean program began in 1999, instituted by the same director who currently runs the program. Since WS operates as a program within Associated Canadian Theological Schools, the one credit Research Strategies course became a requirement for WS as well. Thus it was implemented by 2000 in the WS program, with a goal of enabling WS students to become reasonably competent researchers in their field. The director of the program is highly supportive of information literacy and has always been determined that his students do well. The fledgling online version of the course was chosen as most practical logistically for the WS group. We have never had problems with WS students' computer skills, so taking the course online was not in itself a barrier to success.

As we were about to institute the Research Strategies course for WS in 2000, the WS director asked me to require an actual research paper from his students rather than the research question, annotated outline and bibliography requirement that the final question normally required. This would give WS students an opportunity to write a paper based on solid research, and I would have the opportunity to critique their papers and write extensive notations intended to help them improve their writing skills. While this grading challenge is a heavy one, I do believe the paper-writing requirement is worthwhile to them academically. I could argue that my reading actual research papers is not part of the information literacy educational task, but clearly the paper is the product of the research, and so my critique of it surely helps determine whether or not the research goals have been met.

From the beginning, however, it was obvious that incoming Korean students struggled at a more basic level with the differences between libraries of their previous experience and academic libraries in Canada. Several of them complained, even before the research course cycle began, that they could not learn to do research if they did not understand how Western libraries function. The program director and I felt that doing Research Strategies would be easier for them if we provided them instruction in library use first. Thus we added a prerequisite live, rather than online, Library Skills course in 2000, which was required before students could take Research Strategies. This elicited many expressions of gratitude from WS students, who were not averse to doing extra work if it helped them succeed.

It became clear, however, that despite providing the Library Skills prerequisite, students were finding the following research course a serious challenge. Grades in Research Strategies were low, and levels of understanding of key concepts were not what I expected from graduate students. Clearly, we needed to find better ways of teaching information literacy skills than simply teaching Library Skills as a prerequisite.

So, out of my general ignorance of most things Korean, I went to the director of the program and explained some of the problems his students were experiencing. He was dismayed, and his response was utterly Korean. He told the students that Professor Badke was disappointed with them, and they had to work harder. Now it was my turn to be dismayed. My intention had been to find a way to educate more effectively, not to register my displeasure with my students. Gathering my courage, I went back to the director and assured him that I had not been offended and that the students were indeed working very hard. The task we faced was to find better ways to help them succeed. To his great credit, the director agreed that we had to set a goal to improve what we were doing. As it turned out, however, it was going to be several years before we understood the needs well enough to implement the needed enhancements.

More significant challenges came as research itself became more and more complex. Through the early to middle 2000s, research databases came into their own, demanding increasing levels of sophistication in order to optimize their use. The complexity was not merely in the further bells and whistles available. The increased potential of these databases to narrow to very precise results increased the need for users to be clear and narrowly focused in their searching. Our Korean students could handle the technology, but struggled greatly with getting relevant and focused results from the databases.

Out of concern for their poor search results, I began to look more closely at their research and found a number of things that raised concern. First, students struggled with formulating research questions or problem statements to guide their research. Their questions tended to be too broadly based and too focused on information as a goal rather than information as a tool for problem solving. Thus, they would offer a question like, "What are the main problems facing inner city homeless children?" (broad and intended to see information as goal) rather than, "How can the _____ Program instituted by the City of Vancouver for helping homeless children be enhanced?" (narrower, due to location and type of program, and using information as a tool to solve a problem). My primary response to this difficulty has been to guide and critique the development of research questions over several assignments, sometimes (while feeling awkward doing so) going to the point of suggesting questions that would form a better basis for research.

Second, students struggled with formulating search terminology in English. Not only did they aim too broadly, e.g. "Homelessness," instead of "Homeless children in Vancouver," but at times they lacked the English language skills to formulate sophisticated searches, especially when it came to keyword searching with synonyms. Their struggle with English also made it difficult for them to assess the relevance of the results they found for their original search questions. Even when searches used correct keywords, students tended to accept irrelevant results as relevant. The language challenges were exacerbated in 2008 when specific entrance requirements in English were waived.

Third, most of our common conventions of constructing research papers were quite alien to most of our Worldview Studies students, despite their often-long years of university study in Korea. When the educational emphasis in Korea rests on accumulating a knowledge base more than advancing the knowledge base, many of the skills Westerners expect of their graduate students are not well understood by Korean students. Their abilities to memorize and to understand the content of their fields of study are, of course, often stronger than those found in Western students, but these skills do not ensure ability to do research in a Western setting.

I concluded that the biggest challenges we were facing in trying to turn these students into researchers on the Western model were the large differences in our educational philosophies. It took several years to reach this conclusion and several more to work out an answer. First, I got the assurance of the program director that he did, indeed, want his students to learn a Western approach to informational research. Second, I suggested that we revamp the Library Skills prerequisite, making it a course that included library skills, but also provided an introduction to Western education and to Western style research papers. Once again, to his credit, the director agreed, and in 2006, six years into the program, we upgraded Library Skills to a more comprehensive prerequisite Introduction to Research.

The new Introduction to Research course is taught in two afternoons (8 total hours) at the beginning of the Spring semester, using a Korean translator to ensure that instruction is understood, followed in the same semester by the online Research Strategies. The translator for the Introduction course comes from the staff of the WS program so that no additional cost for translators is incurred. The course is accompanied by an extensive set of assignments intended to provide, not only practice in using our library, but a significant opportunity for students to think through the implications of our educational philosophy, as well as best practices for constructing a research paper (Badke 2011b). Students do have a textbook (Badke 2003), though it is intended to serve more as a reference source for issues they may encounter than as a document they must read and absorb.

There are three sections to the Introduction to Research course: Library Skills, Introduction to Western Educational Philosophy, and a Research Paper Seminar. The library skills component of the course is taught primarily through computer demonstration, but the accompanying assignment has students interacting directly with the physical library as well as practicing searches in the catalog and databases. The students find even the introductory course's assignments very difficult, so we cannot add more workload to increase their skill levels with using the library. Yet double or even triple the practice they are receiving would certainly better prepare them for the Research Strategies course that follows.

The educational philosophy component (Badke 2010d) looks at non-Western as opposed to Western approaches to higher education in a non-judgmental way, stressing that no educational system is better than another; they are "just different." It considers Western critical thinking from the standpoint of asking good questions and identifying the best evidence to support an argument. Throughout this part of the Introduction prerequisite, the role of information as a tool rather than a goal is viewed as resting at the heart of Western educational philosophy. In their assignments, students are asked to assess problems and arguments from a Western point of view, analyzing them and suggesting ways of approaching them critically.

The research paper component is similar to what many students receive in a research paper-writing workshop, but the emphasis is on developing problem-oriented research questions and using information as a tool. Many of our WS students, though working at the graduate level, have written few actual research papers, so even the basics of structure and intent are significant instructional components. Instructional takeaway content is provided through a PowerPoint (Badke 2010e) and a web page (Badke 2009).

Sample Assignments in the Introduction to Research Course

Example 1. For each of the following classification numbers, find the area of the library where that classification number is located and write down the subject of the books with that number.

D568.4	BX3503	BL2747.3	
BR600	R726.8	HE401	E96.2

Example 2. You are writing a paper on an issue in Christian ethics of assisted suicide and you disagree with some of your fellow students about your ethical position. Do you:
- O   i. Write only about your point of view, persuading the reader that you are right, but not dealing with the other views?
- O   ii. Describe all the points of view and leave the conclusion up to the reader?
- O   iii. Find out from your professor what the correct view is and write only in support of that view.
- O   iv. Evaluate the evidence for and against each point of view and choose the one that you believe has the best evidence?

Example 3. Suggest three possible research questions for the following situation. Indicate which of the three questions you think is the best one:

In 2003, a coalition of American and British forces invaded Iraq to destroy the regime of Saddam Hussein. Saddam has now been captured and executed, and Western forces are seeking to move the country toward a democratic system. At the same time, much fighting continues, many Western soldiers have been killed, and there are fears of civil war when the Western forces leave.

Possible research questions:
i.
ii.
iii.

Overall, despite all the effort we have put to improving WS student research skills, I have been less than satisfied with the results of the Introduction to Research prerequisite course. While the concept continues to appear appropriate, and the director of the Worldview Studies program is enthusiastic about it, the profound differences in educational philosophy that we are dealing with are not readily solved by a two-day course and a set of assignments. For students steeped in an authoritarian educational system within which learning is based more on memorization than on critical discovery, making the transition to a Western approach is not easy. It is not that they are resistant to doing so, but that it is difficult for them to grasp what is expected of them. In the realm of research, the biggest hurdle for them to overcome is moving from the idea of information as the goal of their quest to information as a tool intended to solve a problem. When that is paired with their minimal experience in doing informational research, and the program's removal of a minimal English language requirement, they do indeed have a struggle.

When WS students subsequently take the one credit online Research Strategies course (Badke 2010a), the challenges they face, even with the prerequisite Introduction to Research course, are almost legendary. I am constantly told by WS students themselves, and by the program director, that research is "very difficult" for them, and that I need to be understanding. Success in the course is measured by rubrics attached to assignments and ultimately both by existing standards of information literacy, such as the ACRL Competency Standards and my own knowledge of the skill levels required for graduate study at my institution. I am thus well able to determine whether or not students are succeeding. Success, unfortunately, continues to be more limited than what I find with Western-born students.

While I do believe that the prerequisite course helps, I have become increasingly aware that it is not enough. Thus we have begun instituting further aids. Since 2009, the Worldview Studies program has begun optimizing a useful trait in Korean students—their tendency to collaborate. While collaboration can be detrimental when it means that the more able students carry the less able ones, WS has taken another direction. A study group was instituted that goes over every Research Strategies assignment as well as required readings and enables students to achieve consensus as to what is expected. The group does its work in its native Korean language under the guidance of a well-educated WS staff member, and the collaborative effort appears to be helping. The person who leads the group has served as a translator in the prerequisite Introduction to Research course and is able to guide students through the Research Strategies course material. While it may be argued that these students are getting too much help for work they should be doing themselves, I argue that we are merely overcoming obstacles to learning and skill development.

In 2010, Worldview Studies translated the textbook being used for the online Research Strategies course (Badke 2011a) into a shorter web version in Korean (Badke 2010b). Syllabi and other course materials were also translated. These efforts will provide students with the key concepts in their own language. It would also be beneficial to have the entire textbook, for which a new edition in English is to be released in early 2011, translated into Korean.

While a case study such as this one should ideally be a success story, success is still rather elusive. On the plus side, we are gradually removing many of the challenges to understanding the content, whether it is textbook content or assignment requirements. WS students are happy with the prerequisite Introduction to Research course and have declared it helpful. We are also seeing some improvement in student work within the online Research Strategies course.

Conclusion

One might ask, "Why is the library so heavily invested in the education of one group of students?" The simple answer is that the parent institution, Associated Canadian Schools of Trinity Western University, mandates this level of effort, just as it mandates credit-bearing information literacy instruction for all of its students. The Worldview Studies effort is, thus, not alien to the goals of the entire institution, just rather more difficult to implement. At a deeper level, both the director of the Worldview Studies program and the nature of the program itself demand students who can handle information well, critically think through competing ideas, and write effectively and convincingly. Thus information literacy is embedded in the ethos of the program and its director is insistent that his students become information literate.

Are we accomplishing our goals? I would have to admit that we are doing so only partially, though not for lack of effort. Having revised our methods over a number of years, I believe that the problem is less methodology than a struggle to overcome the immense hurdles preventing our graduate Korean students from transitioning from one approach to education to another, while at the same time achieving graduate level skills. These students are bright and teachable, but there is much to assimilate, and one semester of programming through a prerequisite and a graduate level research course does not appear to be enough.

Potential further efforts could include more information literacy coursework or revision/addition to the existing one semester program. The former is not likely to succeed, both because of curricular time limitations and the fact that any further existing courses in which information literacy could be embedded are generally taught in Korean and would not lend themselves easily to having English language information literacy modules added to them.

There is, however, some potential for further development. One avenue we have long sought is to teach the entire information literacy component in Korean, using course textbooks and other materials that are translated into Korean. At this point, however, we have not been able to identify a Korean-speaking professional academic librarian to do the teaching and grading.

A more feasible approach may be to translate the main textbook (Badke 2011a) into Korean. It might also be possible to have students write assignments in Korean and have them translated, or even to use computer translation. Several database companies, such as EBSCO, are currently providing foreign language interfaces to aid students, even though search terms and results will generally be in English.

The Worldview Studies project in many ways has been an experiment in how far an academic library can extend itself to enable international students to meet program goals. Our case may be somewhat extreme, but it reveals both the opportunities and the limitations of such efforts.

References

Badke, William. 2002. "International Students: Information Literacy or Academic Literacy?" *Academic Exchange Quarterly* 6 (2): 60-65.

Badke, William. 2003. *Beyond the Answer Sheet: Academic Success for International Students.* New York: iUniverse.

Badke, William. 2009. "Writing Research Essays: A Guide for Students of All Nations." http://acts.twu.ca/Library/research_essays.htm.

Badke, William. 2010a. "RES 500 OL, Research Strategies: A One Credit Graduate Level Interactive Course in Information Research Skills. http://acts.twu.ca/Library/research500.htm.

———. 2010b. "Research Strategies (abridged)." http://acts.twu.ca/Library/preface.htm.

———. 2010c. "Syllabus: RES 500 A (Research Strategies)." http://acts.twu.ca/Library/RES500ASyllabus.pdf.

———. 2010d. "Western Education & Critical Thinking [PowerPoint]." http://www.scribd.com/doc/40279229/Western-Education-Critical-Thinking.

———. 2010e. "Writing Research Papers: A Presentation by William Badke [PowerPoint]." http://www.scribd.com/doc/40419991.

Badke, William. 2011a. *Research Strategies: Finding your Way through the Information Fog*, 4th ed. New York: iUniverse.

———. 2011b. "Syllabus: RES 490 Introduction to Research." http://acts.twu.ca/Library/RES490Spring2011.pdf.

Cho, Sookyung. 2010. "Academic Biliteracy Challenges: Korean Scholars in the United States." *Journal of Second Language Writing* 19 (2): 82-94.

Kwon, Sung-Ho and P.A. Danaher. 2001. "Comparing Korean and Australian Open and Distance Higher Education: The Social Control Social Capital Continuum and Pendulum." *Asia Pacific Education Review* 1 (1): 115. http://eri.snu.ac.kr/aper/pdf/1-1/11-Sung-Ho%20Kwon.pdf.

Lee, Jeong-Kyu. 2001. "Confucian Thought Affecting Leadership and Organizational Culture of Korean Higher Education." *Radical Pedagogy* 3 (3). http://radicalpedagogy.icaap.org/content/issue3_3/5-lee.html.

Roslyn Kunin & Associates, Inc. 2009. *Economic Impact of International Education in Canada: Final report. Presented to: Foreign Affairs and International Trade Canada*. Vancouver, BC: Roslyn Kunin & Associates, Inc. http://www.international.gc.ca/education/assets/pdfs/RKA_IntEd_Report_eng.pdf

Young, Jeffrey R. 2010. "S. Korean Colleges Aim to Prosper in Worldwide Online Education." *Chronicle of Higher Education* September 21, 2010. http://chronicle.com/article/S-Korean-Colleges-Aim-to/124558/?sid=wc&utm_source=wc&utm_medium=en.

Chapter 11
Connecting@ZSR: Meeting the Research Needs of International Graduate Students

Sarah H. Jeong and H. David "Giz" Womack

The Z. Smith Reynolds Library at Wake Forest University has been working to unify and strengthen its role in Graduate Student Orientation in an effort to better meet the needs of these students, recognizing that graduate students have different research needs than undergraduate students. Graduate Student Orientation activities include technology orientation, orientation for graduate teaching assistants, orientation for new Divinity School students and a brief orientation for international graduate students. The Research and Instruction Librarian for Science solicited the support of the Instruction and Outreach Librarian and the Center for International Studies to collaborate on an expanded role for the Library in the International Graduate Student Orientation. Along with the existing technology orientation and brief library orientation for international graduate students, two new programs were created, "Connecting@ZSR" and "Researching@ZSR." These programs offer more in-depth library orientation and research instruction. As with any new program, there were many challenges along the way and lessons learned upon completion of the program.

Introduction

Wake Forest University offers Ph.D. programs in the sciences and master's degree programs in various disciplines in the humanities, social sciences, and sciences. Since international graduate students, for the most part, do not attend undergraduate college in the United States, they are a unique part of the student population with special research needs. The Instruction and Outreach Librarian and the Research and Instruction Librarian for Science initiated a library orientation program to connect international graduate students with library services and librarians.

The authors conducted a needs assessment with the Center for International Studies, and a literature search of similar programs at other universities during the development of the library orientation program for international graduate students. Baron and Strout-Dapaz (2001) surveyed academic libraries in the southern United States and recommended a model for library skills training for international students based on the Association of College and Research Libraries (ACRL) Information Literacy Competency Standards. Their model covered critical library skills for international students including the organization of information in the Library of Congress (LC) or Dewey classification systems, research aids with modular tutorials that offer point-of-need training, copyright, plagiarism, and citations.

The authors developed two outreach programs: "Connecting@ZSR" and "Researching@ZSR." "Connecting@ZSR" provided a tour of the library to show various services and to introduce the international graduate students to other Research and Instruction Librarians and Library staff. The second program, "Researching@ZSR," involved a one-hour library instruction session, which covered searching the library catalog and databases, accessing journals, Toolkit video tutorials, plagiarism, citations, and electronic theses and dissertations.

The Institution

Wake Forest University is a private university in North Carolina, founded in 1834 with a unique educational mission: it seeks to build not only intellect, but also character. The University believes deeply in its responsibility to educate the whole person—mind, body, and spirit—and to help students find their place in the world following graduation. The Reynolda Campus, the university's main campus, was relocated to north of downtown Winston-Salem in 1956. The Wake Forest School of Medicine is located on the Bowman Gray campus. The University's Babcock Graduate School of Management maintains a presence on the main campus in Winston-Salem and in Charlotte, North Carolina.

In the 2009 *U.S. News and World Report* America's Best Colleges report, Wake Forest ranked 28th overall among national universities. Additionally, the same report ranked Wake Forest University 11th overall in terms of Best Undergraduate Teaching among national universities. In the 2009 *BusinessWeek* Undergraduate Business Schools Rankings, the Calloway School of Business and Accountancy was ranked 14th overall, and 1st in terms of Academic Quality.

In Fall 2009, Wake Forest University's overall student enrollment was 7,079, including 2,510 graduate and professional school students (Wake Forest University 2009). Two hundred and thirty-five international students, 171 of them graduate students, from 50 different countries attended Wake Forest (Wake Forest University Center for International Studies 2009).

The Initiatives

In the Summer of 2009, the librarians began an initiative to raise awareness among graduate students regarding the research services available at the Z. Smith Reynolds Library. This included library outreach to the international students by means of participating in the International Graduate Student Orientation in August 2009. In the Summer of 2010, the Library decided to expand this program and play a larger role in the orientation of international graduate students. The librarians conducted a needs assessment with Kent Greer, Assistant Director for International Students and Scholars, at Wake Forest University. The results of the needs assessment indicated the need to educate international students about finding scholarly information sources not readily available on the Internet and clarifying what constitutes plagiarism in the United States.

Based on the international students' needs assessment (Appendix A), the librarians created two programs, "Connecting@ZSR" and "Researching@ZSR." "Connecting@ZSR" included speaking at the International Graduate Student Orientation and having students meet with H. David "Giz" Womack, Instruction and Outreach Librarian, and Sarah Jeong, Research and Instruction Librarian for Science. The program also included a tour of the Library and an introduction to other research and instruction librarians and library staff. The second program, "Researching@ZSR," focused on literature searching in databases, accessing electronic journals, interlibrary loan, introducing students to the social media tools such as the Library's Facebook fan page and Toolkit videos that offer instruction using library services, and discussing the concept of plagiarism in the United States. After the completion of these two programs, these international graduate students were sent an electronic survey to assess the usefulness of and user satisfaction with the programs.

International Graduate Student Orientation

In late August of 2010, the librarians participated in the International Graduate Student Orientation. With only ten minutes carved out of an already full day of orientation speakers and events, it was important to deliver a carefully crafted message that focused on accessing the library's services and encouraging the students to attend the two in-depth sessions "Connecting@ZSR" and "Researching@ZSR." The program focused on three areas: the library website, the library as a place, and the upcoming opportunity to meet with librarians in the library's Starbucks.

The URL for the library's website (http://zsr.wfu.edu) and three key resources available on the website were featured in the presentation: Interlibrary Loan, the study room reservation system, and personal research sessions or PRSs. The idea was to highlight resources of particular use to graduate students beyond the traditional demonstration of a database, since time was limited and database searching would be covered later in the "Researching@ZSR" program. Locations in the Library that are of particular use to graduate students were discussed. Obtaining a graduate student study carrel, reserving study rooms online, and finding "The Bridge" (aka, the Information Systems Service Desk) for technology support were covered. Graduate students at Wake Forest get 250 free pages of printing each semester, and how to access those free pages and use the networked, multifunction copier, scanner and printers in the Library was discussed. In addition to covering resources to support scholarly pursuits, the presentation also covered how to check out popular DVDs from the library media collection, and ended with the students using "clickers" (an audience response system) to select the best date for the next follow-up program "Connecting@ZSR." The librarians gave out business cards and candy to the students as the session ended and encouraged them to attend the upcoming sessions.

Graduate Student Technology Orientation

On the Tuesday following our library orientation session with the international graduate students, the Instruction and Outreach Librarian led a technology orientation session for all graduate students, including the international graduate students. Most graduate students at Wake Forest University get a two-year-old Lenovo ThinkPad as part of their graduate program. Ph.D. students receive a new Lenovo ThinkPad. These laptops have been previously used by undergraduates who get a new laptop as a freshman at Wake Forest, which they use until they are beginning their junior year when they turn it in for another new laptop. Upon graduating they return the second laptop. The purpose of these laptops is to offer students access to a standard software load. The University negotiates licensing for software ranging from the latest version of Microsoft Office to academic applications like EndNote for managing citations and discipline-specific applications like Maple for math and modeling.

While undergraduate students participate in an online technology orientation, international graduate students, like all graduate students at Wake Forest, attend a technology orientation after receiving the Lenovo ThinkPad that is led by the Instruction and Outreach Librarian. This session was designed to cover computing at Wake Forest, specifically as it relates to graduate students who are more likely to access University resources from-off campus. During this session, the Scholarly Communications Librarian described the Wake Forest open access repository, WakeSpace, where students will submit their thesis or dissertation online, and introduced them to "PROACT: Your Career Starts Now," a professional development series co-sponsored by the Z. Smith Reynolds Library and the Graduate School Professional Development Advisory Committee. This series hosts events covering content important for the overall development of professionals that may not be addressed through graduate course work.

In order to introduce both domestic and international graduate students to the technology resources they need to succeed at Wake Forest, the graduate student technology orientation covered a wide range of topics. The program began with basics such as login and password conventions, ensuring everyone could log onto the campus network and access Internet resources. This was also a time when any mechanical issues with the Lenovo ThinkPad could be addressed as well as instructions on care of the ThinkPad and warranty information. Once these students could login and connect, it was important to review connecting to the campus wireless network and how to use the VPN (virtual private network) to access campus resources such as library databases from off-campus. Topics such as Gmail and the Wake Forest Intranet were covered, and time was spent on backing up files, specifically theses and dissertation files. How to get help from the Information Systems Service Desk, in-person and online, were discussed, as were the workshops available through the Professional Development Center at Wake Forest. These students, who often live off-campus, needed to be made aware of the campus resources available to them that they might otherwise miss as non-residential students.

"Connecting@ZSR"

Later in August of 2010, the librarians met with international graduate students at the library's Starbucks, and then led a tour of the Library. Since Physics graduate students were required to attend a safety-training workshop on August 24th, many international graduate students had a scheduling conflict with the tour. Unfortunately, when selecting a time for "Connecting@ZSR," these students were unaware of the date and time of the safety-training workshop. In the future, the librarians will work with the Center for International Studies to ensure there is no conflict. The goal of this session was to introduce the international graduate students to other librarians and library services available to them. Library services, including the Circulation Desk and Reference Desk were highlighted, in addition to Current Periodicals and the Information Systems Service Desk, aka "The Bridge." Printing and photocopying in the Library were also demonstrated. In addition, the students were shown the main stacks and study rooms in the Library. During the tour, the students asked for help with searching the library catalog for books for their graduate studies, and the librarians showed them the public computers in the Reference Department and provided tips for navigating the library catalog. At the end of the tour, the students were also shown where the librarians' offices were located to encourage them to visit in the future.

"Researching@ZSR"

Scheduling the follow-up session to "Connecting@ZSR" proved to be a challenge. In an effort to avoid any scheduling conflicts, the Center for International Studies was contacted and with their input, Thursday, September 30, 2010 at 6:00 p.m. was selected for the one-hour session. Prior to the session, one of the librarians created an online research guide for the international students using LibGuides (http://guides. zsr.wfu.edu/international). Additionally, students were notified of this session via email from the Center for International Studies and were encouraged to bring their ThinkPad laptops to the program in order to make it a hands-on session. Six students attended the session.

The session began with an in-depth look at research resources available via the library's website. The librarians began the session by encouraging them to "Like" the Z. Smith Reynolds Library on Facebook, and then showed them how to access the research guide designed to assist them with their research. In addition to instruction on using the library catalog, the students were shown how to search by call number and how to access WorldCat. After reviewing how to find books in the Library, we moved on to accessing the library databases for finding scholarly journal articles. Both general and subject specific databases were discussed, as were online dictionaries and a glossary of library terminology. Links to all the resources covered in the session were available via the LibGuide created for these students. The library's website and the LibGuide were the focus of the research instruction session.

The section on plagiarism covered intellectual property, rights of the copyright owner, and ways to avoid plagiarism by citing sources. Clickers and Turning Point software were used to receive anonymous, informal feedback on questions related to intellectual property issues (Appendix B). The Assistant Director for Research and Instruction, Rosalind Tedford, developed these questions. The students were also introduced to citation management software applications such as EndNote and Zotero. Students were told how to access this software and when workshops were available on these applications. As in the graduate student technology orientation, submitting electronic theses and dissertations to the institutional repository was discussed, but in this session there was also time to view the repository and tell the students more about the process. The "PROACT: Your Career Starts Now," a professional development series co-sponsored by the Z. Smith Reynolds Library and the Graduate School Professional Development Advisory Committee, was also mentioned again and the students were shown how to sign up for the workshops on the Professional Development Center website.

At the end of the "Researching@ZSR," the students were sent a link to a survey of the sessions where they could offer feedback on the library's research instruction session for international graduate students. The students were then introduced to the research and instruction librarian on duty that evening and shown the Graduate Student Lounge housed in the Library.

Survey

Before the survey on the usefulness of the library orientation was administered to the international graduate students, the study needed approval from the Institutional Review Board (IRB). The authors completed the Collaborative IRB Training Initiative (CITI) Basic Human Subjects Research course and received certification. Topics covered during CITI training included an overview of regulations applied to social and behavioral science research, assessing risk in human subject research, informed consent, privacy, confidentiality, and financial conflicts of interest in research involving human subjects. Since the anonymity of the international graduate students who participated in the library instruction program and completed the survey was maintained, there was minimal risk to the participants, and the authors' research study application was approved by the IRB with exempt status.

A link to the online survey was distributed via email to the international students after attending "Researching@ZSR." E-mail reminders were sent 4 days and 12 days after the initial invitation to the survey. Five out of six attendees replied to the survey, giving a response rate of 83%.

The questionnaire mainly focused on evaluating the Graduate Student Orientation, the library instruction session, and library services, including seven Likert scale questions and three short answer questions. Question 3 was converted from a 6-point Likert scale to a 5-point scale for consistency. The international graduate students' responses are summarized in Table 11.1.

Although the authors did not consider statistical analysis because of the small sample size, students' overall responses were very positive, which implies that although this program was the first attempt at Wake Forest University, it was well organized and helpful for the international graduate students. All survey respondents agreed that the ZSR Library section of the Graduate Student Orientation and library orientation were useful to them. However, the library instruction session needs to be re-examined since plagiarism and the ethical and legal issues related to information use received one negative response.

Table 11.1. Library instruction session survey for international graduate students at Wake Forest University

Questionnaire	Strongly agree	Agree	Neutral	Disagree	Strongly disagree
1. The ZSR Library section of graduate student orientation in August 2010 was useful to me.	3	2			
2. The ZSR Library instruction session in September 2010 was useful to me.	3	2			
3. Please rank the topics covered during the ZSR Library instruction in Sept. 2010 that were most helpful to you					
a. Plagiarism in the United States			1		1
b. Databases & accessing e-journals online and through Interlibrary Loan	2	1			
c. Endnote/Zotero			3		
d. Submitting electronic theses & dissertations (ETDs)		1		1	
e. Social media tools (ZSR Library Facebook fan page)	1		1		1
f. Toolkit video tutorials	2	1		1	
	Responses				
4. Overall, what did you find MOST valuable about the Library section of graduate student orientation in September 2010 and why?	1. I liked it very much. 2. There is a separated study space for graduate students.				
5. Overall, what did you find LEAST valuable about the Library section of graduate student orientation in August, and/or the Library instruction session in September 2010 and why?	3. Everything is the most important and they are quite helpful for me. 4. Most of the information are useful				
6. How should the Library orientation and/or Library instruction session for international graduate students be improved in the future?	5. It's already very well designed, I hope this can be done much earlier. 6. Show them the structure of library				

Table 11.1. Library instruction session survey for international graduate students at Wake Forest University

	Strongly agree	Agree	Neutral	Disagree	Strongly disagree
7. Would you recommend the Library orientation session held in August 2010 as part of graduate student orientation to other international graduate students?	1	3			
8. Would you recommend the library instruction session, held in ZSR Library in Sept. 2010, to other international graduate students?	2	3			
9. As a result of this library orientation and/or library instruction session I am more likely to ask for assistance when using library services/ resources.	2	2	1		
10. ZSR Library has appropriate services/resources to support my graduate studies.	3	2			

Endnote and Zotero, Electronic Theses and Dissertations (ETDs), and social media tools (ZSR Library Facebook fan page) received neutral responses overall. One student commented that what he/she found to be the most valuable aspect of the library orientation was the Graduate Student Lounge, which is a separate study space for graduate students. Two students answered that most of the information presented at the September 2010 "Researching@ZSR" session was useful and helpful. In response to the question about how the library orientation could be improved in the future, one student commented that he/she preferred that the library orientation be scheduled earlier in the semester. Another student answered that they would like to see the structure of the library, which can be interpreted as a tour of the library.

Conclusion

The survey results indicate that the outreach program was successful in providing a library orientation program for incoming international graduate students. The library instruction sessions may need to be improved based on the small percentage of negative and neutral responses. However, the librarians received positive responses and constructive criticism overall. Lessons learned include the importance of scheduling events that are held early in the semester and that do not conflict with any other required orientation events. Also, consolidating events into the fewest number possible while still meeting the needs of the students would be useful. In the future, combining "Connecting@ZSR" and "Researching@ZSR" into one session would ease the scheduling burden on all participants. Additionally, while this increased contact with the international graduate students made the cultural differences more apparent, it also gave the librarians the opportunity to overcome those differences by creating relationships with these students. Based on the user satisfaction, the librarians plan to make this program a part of the international graduate student orientation each year. Another lesson learned came in meeting the IRB requirements. In order to be in compliance, the librarians had to commit to the time required to complete the CITI course and submit their survey for review, which also proved to be a more challenging task than first thought. While going through the IRB process was an overall positive experience, it proved more time consuming than expected. This was the first time that the library outreach program was offered to the international graduate students, and the authors will reflect on the students' honest feedback in the development of the library orientation program in the future.

References

Baron, S., and A. Strout-Dapaz. 2001. Communicating with and empowering international students with a library skills set. *Reference Services Review* 29 (4): 314–326.

Wake Forest University Center for International Studies. 2009. "Wake Forest University International Student Statistics, Fall 2009."

Wake Forest University. 2009. "Discover Wake Forest." Accessed January 28, 2011. http://admissions.wfu.edu/discover/facts.php

Appendix A: Needs Assessment Questions

1. What are important information needs of international students?

2. Which library services are critical for the academic success of international students that they should be aware of?

3. What else can the library offer to help international students succeed?

Appendix B: Can You Do That?
A Quiz on Intellectual Property Issues

1. You are writing a research paper for your Art History class. You ask your roommate to proofread it for you. Is this....
   O Cheating
   O Not Cheating

2. On the first day of classes you are happy to discover the final paper is on a topic you wrote a paper on last term. You print off a new copy and hand it in on the due date with a new cover page.
   O Plagiarism
   O Not Plagiarism

3. You are supposed to have 9 sources for a paper. You only use 7 in your research, so you enter in 2 additional sources you didn't actually use in your bibliography.
   O Cheating
   O Not Cheating

4. As you are writing a paper, you copy and paste into MS Word from different online journals, books and web pages. You go back and reword a lot of what you copied and rearrange the information so it makes sense. Since you have changed a good percentage of what you brought into your paper, you decide not to cite the sources.
   O Plagiarism
   O Not Plagiarism

5. It's the night before a paper is due and you have a quote in your paper that is really good, but you can't find the book or article where you got it. You decide to pass the quote off as your own idea and not cite it. It's just one quote, after all. Is this...
   O Plagiarism
   O Not Plagiarism

6. You buy a CD from Best Buy. You take it home and make a copy of it for your car and you rip it to play on your MP3 player.
    O Copyright Violation
    O Not a Copyright Violation

7. It is the night before graduation and you are having a party for your best friends in graduate school. You decide to make a mixed CD of all the songs that you loved while in school with these people. You make a copy of the CD for each person at the party as a gift.
    O Copyright Violation
    O Not a Copyright Violation

8. You buy a CD from Best Buy but your ripping software isn't working. So you go online and download the songs for free from someone else via MyTunes, Morpheus, Limewire, Bitorrent, or eDonkey
    O Copyright Violation
    O Not a Copyright Violation

9. You are doing a presentation on product placement in movies and TV shows in a marketing class. You rip scenes off of DVDs to show to make your point that advertisers are using this method of advertising.
    O Copyright Violation
    O Not a Copyright Violation

10. You do a paper on the history of Hip-Hop. On the cover page you insert an image from Amazon of the cover of a Hip Hop album.
    O Copyright Violation
    O Not a Copyright Violation

Chapter 12

An Integrated Approach to Supporting International Students at the University of Technology, Sydney in Australia

Dr. Alex Byrne

The University Library at the University of Technology (UTS), Sydney in Australia has long supported internationalization. Its integrated programs support both international students coming to study in Australia and Australian-based UTS students going to study in other countries. Initiatives include a team of specialist librarians, Chinese language web pages, resources in many languages, guides in the languages other than English most frequently spoken by students, an innovative International Cultural and News Centre, information literacy programs offered in Chinese, and cultural awareness training for all library staff. This program is unusual in its breadth and integrated nature. It supports a burgeoning number of international students drawn from many nations to study in Australia. The paper traces the development of these integrated programs and situates them within the extraordinarily successful attraction of international students to Australian universities.

Introduction

Over the last twenty years, Australian universities have been extraordinarily successful in attracting students from other countries to study at universities in Australia and on campuses of Australian universities located in other countries. Australian curricula have also been offered by partner institutions in other countries and, to a more limited extent, through distance education. The export of higher education services, as economists describe it, has had major consequences for Australian universities, including their libraries, which have sought to support international students wholeheartedly.

Responding to the needs of international students has been challenging because of the diversity of their origins and their varied educational preparation for study in Australia, often including limited exposure to modern academic libraries and sometimes-poor English language skills. These issues and others have been recognized at the University of Technology, Sydney where the University Library has taken a broad approach to internationalization and progressively developed a highly integrated approach to supporting international students.

Cultural Context
A Major Export Industry: International Students in Australia
Australia is the world's third most popular English-speaking destination for university study, and the fifth most popular overall—behind the United States, United Kingdom, Germany and France (Australian Government, Department of Education, Employment and Workplace Relations 2011). Approximately 491,500 students from 190 countries enrolled in courses in Australia in 2009, giving the country the most international students per capita of population. University enrollments increased by 12% in 2009 to 203,300 of whom 24% came from China, 18% from India, 6% from the Republic of Korea with 71% coming from the top 10 nations (China, India, Korea, Malaysia, Thailand, Vietnam, Nepal, Indonesia, Brazil and USA) (Australian Education International 2011b). More than three-quarters chose to study in Australia without applying to any other countries (Varghese and Brett 2011).

International education earned the Australian economy AUD 19.1 billion (USD 19.3 billion) in 2009-10, 10.2 % more than the AUD 17.1 billion in 2008-09 (Australian Education International 2011a). Even though this excluded earnings from overseas campuses of Australian universities, this performance made education Australia's largest services export industry ahead of other personal travel services (AUD 12.1 billion) and professional and management consulting services (AUD 3.1 billion). Of the total export income generated by education services, universities generated AUD 10.6 billion (57.4%), vocational and technical education AUD 5.1 billion (27.7%), English language courses AUD 1,033 million (5.6%), schools AUD 852 million (4.6%), and non-award AUD 597 million (3.2%).

These figures bear quoting because they demonstrate not only the marked success of Australian international education, but also show that it is led by universities since they dominate the income, and also provide the attraction for students to complete their schooling in Australia or to undertake English language or feeder vocational courses in Australia. It also highlights the crucial importance of the income from international students' fees to the financial bottom line for Australian universities.

A government website (Australian Government, Department of Education, Employment and Workplace Relations 2011) claims that international students choose to study in Australia because Australian schools, colleges and universities offer a high quality of education, Australia is a safe and secure place to live, it offers the experience of a new culture and lifestyle and it is possible to live close to a beautiful natural environment. These claims are broadly true, but the market for students from India was rocked in 2010 by several attacks on Indian students in Australia. Early enrollment data for 2011 indicates that demand from India is down although it is acknowledged that recent changes to criteria for student visas have also had a dampening effect.

In spite of that current setback in the Indian market, international education has been a tremendous success story, which has had major implications for Australian universities. Australia has the highest proportion of overseas university students of all OECD countries—19.3 percent in 2005 compared to the OECD average of 7.2 percent (Australian Government, Department of Education, Employment and Workplace Relations 2008). In 2006, 13 Australian universities had over 8,000 international students (including both onshore and offshore enrollments) and three had more than 16,000 (Monash University, RMIT University, Curtin University). In contrast, the U.S. university with the largest international enrollment at a comparable time, University of Southern California, had just over 7,000 international students.

These large numbers of culturally diverse students are unevenly distributed both across and within universities. The most popular state for overseas students is New South Wales, where the University of Technology, Sydney (UTS) is located (Australian Education International 2011a). That state attracted AUD 6.8 billion or 37 % of the income in 2009-10 and was followed by Victoria (32%) and Queensland (15%). Within the universities, international students are most likely to be found in business courses leading to higher proportions in such courses than the overall average, around 20%, would suggest.

A commonly cited rule of thumb for maintaining an Australian educational experience is to strive for a maximum of 25% international enrollments in a course, but this can be exceeded in popular courses. Such imbalances lead to complaints from international students that they did not come to Australia to study with other 'internationals.' Nevertheless, international students are overall very satisfied with their experience of studying in Australia, including their use of university libraries, which were rated 95% in importance and 83% in satisfaction in a recent survey (Varghese and Brett 2011).

The Institution

Created in 1988, UTS has developed rapidly to become a median sized Australian university. Its programs span engineering, IT, science, nursing, education, business, sport and tourism, design and architecture, law and the humanities and social sciences. Approximately a third of the 32,000 students, and a higher proportion of international students, are studying courses such as accountancy, international business and management through the Faculty of Business. Many domestic students undertake international studies courses, which include a period of up to a year studying at a university in another country for credit toward their UTS degree.

The city campus is located in Sydney's central business district, so it is an extremely urban campus with all the benefits and challenges that entails. It has the buzz of the city, but also some issues with petty crime and extraordinarily expensive accommodation, which often places students in overcrowded shared rooms. A recent advertisement posted outside the University Library, for example, invited international students to apply to share a two-bedroom apartment with four males in one bedroom and four females in the other. This makes it very difficult to study 'at home,' leading to heavy use of the Library and other University facilities.

A second campus is in a beautiful, leafy suburban location, but is unpopular with most students, including international students, because it is away from the urban buzz and lacks good transportation. The University Library is centralized with libraries on each campus, but no departmental or branch libraries.

UTS currently has some 6,000 international students with strong enrollments from: China (41%); Vietnam and India (6% each); Korea, Nepal and the Philippines (5% each); Indonesia (4%); Saudi Arabia, Bangladesh and Iran (2% each); with 21.3% from other countries. The domestic student body is similarly diverse because of the high rates of migration to Australia and the particular concentration of migrants and their children in Sydney. In recent years, many migrants have come from China or the Chinese diaspora in other nations so the proportion of local Chinese speakers is high—perhaps higher because the city campus is located next to Sydney's extensive and growing Chinatown.

Together, this mix provides a stimulating cultural environment for learning and social interaction. For the University Library, it has long provided both challenges and opportunities to which the Library has responded by developing an integrated program which includes: specialized facilities, an international team of librarians, a Chinese website and guides in languages other than English, training programs offered in Chinese, some signage in languages other than English, multilingual collections, a reading program and use of staff language skills.

Specialized Facilities

UTS established an Institute of International Studies in 1994 to create the international studies course for domestic students mentioned above and to promote internationalization of the University in general. At that stage, the number of students from overseas enrolled at UTS was very small, but the University had made a strategic decision to increase the number since it perceived a decline in government funding for Australian students. Growth in international enrollments developed rapidly following the appointment of a Vice President for University Enterprises in 2000, a position that was replaced by a Vice President (International) in 2005, thereby signaling the University's strategic drive.

The University Library responded by creating an International Cultural and News Centre (ICNC) in 1998 to assist students going to other countries to prepare for their year of in-country study and to enable international students in Sydney to stay in touch with their home countries. Over its first decade, the ICNC offered newspapers and magazines from countries of interest together with travel guides to relevant countries, regions and cities. At the beginning of 2008, the ICNC was relocated to a more prominent location with a large 'international' mural and a number of digital viewing pods to enable students to view televised news, current affairs and cultural programs. Both target groups enjoy the extension from print to digital resources.

At the same time, the Library created a complementary Australian Culture Lounge to introduce international students to aspects of Australian culture. Consisting of a comfortable reading area surrounded by Australian literary and history books, the Lounge has operated in a more symbolic than practical fashion by making a statement to students that they are in Australia. It is unlikely that many read the books since international students are overwhelmingly focused on their studies with little time for extra-curricular activities, but they value the facility as a welcoming site of experiencing Australia.

The Initiatives

The International Team

In addition to creating the ICNC in 1998, the Library appointed Ms. Wei Cai, originally from Nanjing, as the International Studies Librarian. A full member of the Information Services Department's team of reference and liaison librarians, Wei energetically set about providing support for the increasing number of international students as well as the local students beginning their adventures in overseas locations. Her professionalism made her a highly valued colleague to the other librarians and a guide and mentor to students. Her fluency in Chinese was valuable because China had become the main source of international students and because many other students, international and domestic, were—and are—of Chinese heritage. However, Wei and her colleagues support students from the immense variety of national and cultural backgrounds that come to UTS, rendering the University Library a cultural haven within the University.

A decade later, two other librarians were added to create a three person team within the Information Services Department and the variety of services was able to be further expanded to provide in depth service from undergraduate orientation through information literacy and specialist classes to support research degree students.

A Reading Program

Although UTS students study in English and are expected to be competent in English when they start, and sufficiently fluent to practice their professions when they leave, many have difficulty with English when they arrive in Sydney. Studies undertaken by the University's English Language and Study Skills Assistance Centre (ELSSA) in 2009 and 2010 demonstrated that an unacceptable proportion of the students could not explain, in intelligible English, a commonplace device such as an automatic bank teller machine. This finding, which is not unique to UTS, has given the University pause and led to the adoption of a much stronger policy on English language and the implementation of strategies to assist students to improve their English skills.

So as to provide a non-threatening means of building students' competence in English, the Library established a reading club in 2010. Starting small, the Reading Club has its own website (http://read.lib. uts.edu.au/p/reading-clubs.html) and Facebook page (http://www. facebook.com/UtsReadingClub) to foster involvement and build a community of readers. Materials read include a Time magazine article on 'Who needs marriage?', 'The Tell-Tale Heart' by Edgar Allan Poe and audio books. Some fun was had with the peculiarities of Australian English, the Australian accent and colloquialisms.

The aim is to create a culture of reading so that students will enjoy reading in English, develop their vocabularies and also make friends. The last aim is important because so many students feel lonely and insecure when studying in a foreign city and culture. The program is firmly rooted in the University Library's roles as the provider of scholarly information and developer of information access skills, but goes further by treating students' needs holistically and recognizing that we can help them adjust to study in Australia by building confidence in one of our core skills, reading.

Assistance in Languages other than English

With a similar aim, the University Library created a subset of its website in Modern Standard Chinese (http://www.lib.uts.edu.au/students/ discover-your-library/chinese-webpages) in 1998 and has since maintained and developed it. This is not to replace the main site, but to provide a welcoming facility for the large proportion of the students who read Chinese, to reduce barriers for them in coming to an English-language university and to make it easy for them to access the support offered by our international team. It also provides an important gateway for students studying UTS courses offshore in China.

In addition, basic Library guides were printed in the most commonly spoken non-English languages including Arabic, Chinese and Thai. The guides offered a gesture of welcome for many of our non-

English background students by acknowledging their languages and cultures. They also opened the door to support for the students and ensured that they could not claim that they were unaware of the libraries policies and facilities, at least at a general level. While not a primary goal in producing the guides, this aspect is of assistance when disciplinary action needs to be taken against students.

In a similar vein, the Library has taken advantage of its multicultural and multilingual staff by inviting staff members to identify the languages in which they feel competent so that they can be called upon if necessary to assist a student. More than 30 languages have been listed, usually with more than one staff member for each, over the last decade. They range from Pashto (Afghanistan) and Farsi (Iran), several Chinese Languages, Vietnamese and Bahasa Malaysia to European languages such as French, Greek and Russian. Demand for assistance is small, but the initiative represents a way in which many members of staff can feel that their particular linguistic skills—and, implicitly, their cultures—are valued and through which they can assist students in times of need.

Some signage is presented in languages other than English, mostly to make a point about the University's multilingualism. However, one particular application is important, the labeling of Silent Study Rooms as 'silent' in all of the most common languages of the University population. A little tongue in cheek, this aims to underline that we really mean the rooms to be silent since the rest of the Library is managed as conversational or quiet areas.

Training Sessions Offered in Chinese

Taking advantage of the Chinese language skills of the international team and recognizing the high proportion of Chinese origin students, the Library has vigorously promoted its services and resources to international students via various channels including its web site, publications and special sessions. It has also integrated Chinese sessions into the library orientation programs, scheduled ever-increasing numbers of workshops in Chinese and it is developing more online tutorials and podcasts to support those students.

The sessions extend from conventional introductory tours to information literacy classes and specific workshops on the use of particular tools such as RefWorks and EndNote. Delivering these sessions in Chinese ensures that students do not fall at the first hurdle when studying their academic programs in English.

At the beginning of the 2011 academic year (they are calendar years in Australia), the University Library mounted an ambitious Research Week, which aimed to provide tool kits for researchers, especially early career researchers and doctoral students. Its subtext was, of course, to signal the centrality of the Library to scholarship and research. Some of the sessions offered during Research Week were also offered in Chinese and a 'Chinese Clinic' was offered to assist doctoral students and researchers from China to navigate the research support offered at UTS by the Library and other units, the Research and Innovation Office in particular.

Multilingual Collections

As well as this extensive range of support programs and multilingual communication media, the University Library has, of course, developed collections in languages other than English. Materials will be purchased in any language required, but there is limited demand except notably from faculty in international studies and in the burgeoning research on China. Research on China is one of the University's strategic areas and consequently the Library has built up respectable collections of research materials, including much in digital form, to support that area.

International studies foci include Italy, Spain and Latin America, France, Germany and Japan. The emphasis at the teaching level is on language and culture, but faculty have their own research interests which tend to be broadly in cultural studies, politics and other social sciences.

The Library also collects some popular materials in the languages of our students to support their recreational needs. These include books, graphic novels and DVDs of films, anime and other video. A small cost item, this again reaches out to students to help them feel secure and able to focus on their learning.

Conclusion

For more than a decade, the University Library at UTS has been building an integrated program of support for international students. The program has sought to address all the facets of the Library's relationships with students in order to build their confidence, develop their skills, including English language skills, and offer ready support.

The program has addressed the environment of the Library, including the development of specialized facilities and the choice of signage. It has included means of communication through printed and online guides and resources. And it has gone to the heart of the Library's purpose in collection development and information literacy.

The evidence of its success lies in the positive feedback received by the University about its Library and in the disproportionate use of the Library by international students. They clearly perceive the University Library to be a haven in which they can feel secure to study in a foreign city, land and culture.

References

Australian Education International. 2011a. "Export Income to Australia from education services in 2009-10." *Research Snapshot.* http://aei.gov.au/AEI/PublicationsAndResearch/Snapshots/2011011401_pdf.pdf.

Australian Education International. 2011b. "International student numbers 2009." *Research Snapshot.* http://aei.gov.au/AEI/PublicationsAndResearch/Snapshots/2010022610_pdf.pdf.

Australian Government. Department of Education, Employment and Workplace Relations. 2011a. "Who, why and what in international education." *Data snapshot.* http://www.deewr.gov.au/International/Pages/Datasnapshot.aspx.

Australian Government. Department of Education, Employment and Workplace Relations. 2008. *Review of Australian Higher Education: discussion paper.* Canberra: DEEWR. http://www.dest.gov.au/NR/rdonlyres/06C65431-8791-4816-ACB9-6F1FF9CA3042/22465/08_222_Review_AusHEd_Internals_100pp_FINAL_WEB.pdf.

Varghese, Mary and Kevin Brett. 2011. *International Student Barometer Project 2010: national report.* Canberra: Universities Australia. http://www.universitiesaustralia.edu.au/resources/817/2011-02%20-%20ISB%20Report+Append_Final.pdf.

Chapter 13
The University of Southern California's Campus-wide Strategies to Reach International Students

Shahla Bahavar, Najwa Hanel, Karen Howell, and Norah Xiao

The University of Southern California (USC) has the largest population of international students in the United States. As one of the key academic units for students' academic success, the USC Libraries have a long history of collaborating with different stakeholders on campus to reach out to these students. USC librarians have developed systematic information service programs in outreach, information literacy and reference services for international students to ensure their special educational and information needs are satisfied and to prepare them to succeed academically. This chapter gives an overview of these campus-wide strategic initiatives and several information literacy programs with different academic departments. It hopes to provide an example of the best practices in the field for other libraries to plan services for their international students.

The Institution

Founded in 1880, the University of Southern California (USC) is a large private research institution located in downtown Los Angeles. The University comprises two campuses: the University Park Campus and the Health Sciences Campus. The University Park Campus (UPC) is home to the USC College of Letters, Arts and Sciences, the USC Graduate School and 17 professional schools. The Health Sciences Campus (HSC) is home to the Keck School of Medicine, the USC

School of Pharmacy and three major teaching hospitals, as well as programs in Occupational Therapy and Physical Therapy. The School of Dentistry and the Dental Library reside on the University Park Campus, and the library is under the jurisdiction of the Associate Dean for Health Sciences Libraries. Also located on the UPC campus, the Law Library serves as an independent library and is governed by a Dean and Associate Dean. In addition, the University has centers in Orange County, Channel Island, Marina Del Rey and Alhambra. The University has a total of 3,300 fulltime and 1,486 part-time faculty as well as 11,500 staff and over 22,300 student employees.

The USC Libraries include 20 libraries and specialized collections at the UPC and HSC campuses. The Libraries are administered by the Dean and the Dean's Cabinet. The Associate Dean for Public Services oversees the activities of the branch libraries and public services operations of the Libraries, including instruction, reference, and access services.

The University's student population has grown to 37,000 which includes 17,500 undergraduate and 19,500 graduate students, who come from all 50 states and 115 countries. Nearly 7,000 international students, around 19 percent of the total student population, are enrolled. According to the 2009–2010 academic year enrollments, the countries with the highest student representation are India, China, Korea, and Taiwan (University of Southern California, Office of International Services 2010). USC is America's leader in international education— a truly international university enrolling more international students than any other university in the United States.

The Office of International Services (OIS) provides support and advising services for international students and scholars. Through the provision of well-designed resources, services and programs, OIS assists international students and scholars to achieve their professional and academic goals and make their association with USC a rewarding experience. OIS provides support services such as assistance with visa applications, financial aid information, general advisement, career services and several other services to facilitate the international students' transition to the United States.

The University has a prominent presence internationally and has established offices in China, Korea, Japan, Hong Kong, Taiwan and Mexico, with the establishment of offices in the Middle East in process. The Office of Globalization, a unit in the Office of the Provost, supervises these overseas offices. Its mission is to support and strengthen the University by creating international academic and research partnerships.

The Initiatives

Partnerships with Key Academic Departments

Due to unfamiliarity with a new culture and academic environment, international students often experience more alienation on campus than other students. Well-designed and implemented information literacy and orientation programs help minimize the sense of alienation and make them feel more at home. These programs help prepare our students to succeed in their academic studies at USC.

The USC Libraries support this endeavor through partnerships with key academic departments, such as the Office of Orientation Programs, the American Language Institute, the Language Academy, and via its own specially designed initiatives.

USC Orientation

The USC Office of Orientation Programs organizes orientation sessions for all incoming USC students, including international students. Attendance is mandatory, except for certain schools that hold their own departmental orientation (Accounting, Business, Dentistry, and Law). International student orientation sessions are held in August before the start of the academic year and in January for students entering mid-year. These two-day sessions include a variety of programs and sessions designed to help students with their transition to USC. Some activities include: opportunities to meet faculty and experience college-level discussions; introductions to USC arts and cultural events; discussions with current students about various involvement opportunities on campus; a chance to speak with representatives from USC Housing, USC Hospitality and USC Transportation; group academic advisement and registration for classes; an opportunity to become acquainted with the Los Angeles community and visit Los Angeles tourist sites; a campus tour hosted by a student Orientation Advisor; and, complete Passport Verification as well as immunization and TB screening.

Library orientation activities are integrated into the two-day long, university-wide International Student Orientation programs administered by the Office of Orientation Programs. These initial orientations enable students to learn what valuable resources and services are available to them at the USC Libraries. Three activities are included: the International Student Resource Fair, Interest Sessions and Library tours.

The USC Office of Orientation Programs hosts an International Student Resource Fair of student services exhibits. Librarians staff the USC Libraries table, greet international students, help them find their subject-specific library and librarian(s), and guide them to library maps, directories, brochures, and other information useful to new students.

Figure 13.1: International Students Resource Fair – USC Libraries Table

These Resource Fairs are very popular with the international students, and are excellent venues for both librarians and international students to meet one another.

A second form of library orientation takes place in the Interest Sessions listed in the mandatory schedule. International students may select from a variety of sessions, including the Library Survival and Research workshops in the library's hands-on computer classrooms. In addition to the handouts from the Resource Fair, students are given more materials on library services and library research, such as services bookmarks (e.g. Ask A Librarian, Off-Campus Access, Online Dissertations and Theses) and other library brochures. Each year the attendance continues to grow, as international students understand the importance of using research libraries in the United States. In August 2010, the Libraries offered 11 orientation sessions to over 1,200 international students.

Because international students come from different cultural and educational backgrounds, they are more vulnerable to feeling lost or confused about using the Western library system (Peters 2010). The USC Libraries orientation sessions introduce international students to the concept of a multi-library system, each with specialized collections and unique services. Since a majority of our international students study science and engineering, learning about the Science & Engineering Library's resources and services and connecting with the librarians specializing in these subject areas facilitates access and eases their information seeking frustration. These sessions also introduce them to other libraries in the system that they might use during their studies at USC.

Some key learning outcomes of the orientation sessions include learning about: a) library locations in the University Park Campus, as well as the Health Sciences Campus; b) the services USC Libraries offer; c) their subject area librarians; d) the USC Libraries catalogs; and e) databases and electronic resources the Libraries have to offer in their area of study. Following a carefully designed orientation program, librarians cover all these aforementioned topics at the Library Survival and Research workshop sections of the international students orientation.

Students leave the orientation events satisfied about the information they learned at the workshops. In Summer 2010, an online assessment of 140 graduate and international students attending library orientation workshops found that they strongly agreed with the following statements: a) this library orientation was valuable; b) this library orientation will benefit my learning experience at USC; and c) they learned a lot about the library that they didn't know before. The top two items students reported they learned during the orientation sessions were knowledge of databases and electronic resources, and services the USC Libraries offer (University of Southern California Libraries 2010)

The third form of library orientation is a library tour. The library tours are one of the most important methods of orienting international students to the physical environment within the library building. International students are often confused about specific library locations, such as book stacks and journal stacks. Of special interest are the branch libraries, where international students will spend a great deal of their time, such as the Doheny Memorial Library (humanities and social sciences), the Science and Engineering Library, and the Leavey Library (24/7 library with Information Commons). Librarians and other professional staff who work at the reference desks provide these tours.

Touring the Doheny Library presents students with an example of a library environment that contains an extensive print collection, multi-floor book and journal stacks, access to the Libraries' special collections and rare book materials, other specialized collections and libraries within the Doheny Library building (Cinema, Music, East Asian), circulation services, and reference desk and research librarians services.

USC has many branch libraries with specialized collections. Attending the Science & Engineering Library tours provides international students with an example of a specialized library. The Science and Engineering librarians orient international students to collection locations, group study spaces, instruction space facilities, and reference and circulation desk services.

Students touring the Leavey Library discover the Information Commons facilities for using multimedia desktops, as well as having convenient access to research librarians and computer consultants. Other services include a Multimedia Commons with scanning and other technology equipment, impressive audiovisual collections and viewing machines, group study rooms, reserve collections and study spaces.

These tours provide appropriate information for international students on where to go for specific services or collections. Specialized brochures and library handouts provide a snapshot of each library's unique resources and services.

American Language Institute

The University of Southern California was one of the first research universities in the nation to establish an English language institute for international students, recognizing that some students might require assistance in order to succeed in their studies. To support such systematic instruction, USC's American Language Institute (ALI) was established in 1959. The ALI is an academic unit under the jurisdiction of the College of Letters, Arts, and Sciences, and consists of 15 faculty members who are committed to the pedagogical mission/vision of the Institute and the University in the teaching of language skills. The focus of the ALI course of study is on pedagogical and process approaches. This means that students learn English through a similar format to learning their first language. In addition, students engage in interactive group activities performing communicative tasks in a learning model that complements ALI's instruction.

Before starting their studies at USC, all new international students are required to take the International Students English Examination. The examination consists of a grammar section, a 40-minute essay, and a 10-minute oral interview. The overall score indicates students' language proficiency and contributes to their language placement profile. Depending on the examination results, students may be required to take between three to twelve hours of English classes per week. The level of classes range from intermediate to advanced in all aspects of English language skills: pronunciation, reading, writing, listening and grammar. ALI also offers a range of elective classes for international students on pronunciation, grammar, dissertation writing and other subjects. All international students enrolled in ALI classes are simultaneously co-enrolled in regular university classes in their area of study.

Over 92% of the international students who are enrolled in ALI classes are graduate students. These students include over 59% in Master's programs, 32.83% in Doctoral programs, and 0.75% in other professional programs. The majority of these graduate students major in engineering with a small percentage in sciences and social sciences. The top areas of study include Electrical Engineering, Computer Science, Industrial and System Engineering, Civil Engineering and Architecture. Undergraduate students comprise 7.13% of the international student population and, unlike the graduate students, their main subject areas are in Economics, Business Administration, and Accounting (University of Southern California, American Language Institute 2010).

Over the years, USC Libraries have established a strong partnership with the American Language Institute. Librarians conduct course-integrated, customized, and interactive information literacy instruction to ALI students in networked computer classrooms. Upon scheduling the session, the librarian teaching the class receives a copy of the students' research prompt as well as further information and other class requirements via direct communication with the faculty.

Librarians design the sessions according to the ACRL information literacy standards as well as the special learning needs of international students. The sessions are designed with active learning approaches and are systematically assessed. Sara Baron and Alexia Strout-Dapaz (2001) recommend a set of information literacy skills specifically for international students that build upon the ACRL Information Literacy Competency Standards. At USC, the public services librarians comply with these standards in teaching international students. The recommended skills include: 1) determining the scope of their information needs, 2) accessing information effectively and efficiently, 3) critically evaluating the sources, 4) incorporating materials into their research assignment, and 5) providing awareness of legal and ethical issues on using information and being informed about plagiarism and citation styles (319).

The USC Libraries offer a rich collection of electronic resources, online databases, e-books, e-journals, and full-text collections. Learning about search strategy, reading and interpreting citations, following steps to retrieve full-text, as well as citing and formatting their paper are all key topics that librarians cover in international students' information literacy sessions.

The sessions are two hours long and cover a wide range of activities. Depending on the ALI faculty, the general themes of the research prompts may vary including, "compare/contrast," "problem/solution," or an issue of choice in the student's field of study. Through hands-on instruction classes, students learn about library research and the information seeking process, as well as search strategy, retrieval, critical thinking, and evaluation skills. The customized information literacy sessions utilize an active learning model tailored to students' class assignments. During the library instruction sessions, students have the opportunity to interact one-on-one with librarians on their specific research topics. This format has proven very effective with many different student learning styles.

The pace of teaching information literacy sessions for international students is slightly different than other library sessions. Brainstorming for keywords and keyword searching, versus searching by subject terms or controlled vocabulary, is a topic that is requested by ALI faculty. Developing synonyms and related terms may also be challenging for international students due to their vocabulary limitations. Clarity in speaking and avoiding library jargon are important factors librarians take into consideration when dealing with international students. Throughout the class presentation, students are encouraged to ask questions. This is a culturally different practice from which most international students are accustomed. The introductory discussions set the stage for librarians to present more advanced instruction on the library research process and then proceed to demonstrate appropriate databases in the students' subject fields.

The group instruction sessions are often followed by interaction at reference desks, one-on-one consultation by appointment, and virtual chat or email reference. To assess student learning and the effectiveness of the instruction sessions, the 3-2-1 survey questionnaire is used, which includes three questions: "three things you learned from the session," "two things you will use from now on" and "one thing you still feel confused about after the session." Librarians take advantage of the collected feedback to enhance the future sessions. Furthermore, a survey tool is used to solicit feedback from the ALI faculty on the librarian's performance. These comments direct librarians' attention to topics not covered, and help them to further customize the library instruction sessions to students' needs.

The Language Academy

The USC Language Academy is affiliated with the USC Rossier School of Education, ranked in the top 25 American schools of education. Unlike the ALI program, students enrolled in the Language Academy have not yet been admitted to USC as registered students in a degree-granting program. Founded in 1993, the Language Academy provides international students with the language skills, academic skills, and cross-cultural understanding they will need to be successful at North American universities. Besides TOEFL (Test of English as a Foreign Language) and ESL (English as a Second Language) classes, the curriculum has both required and elective courses and workshops totaling 21 study hours per week. The Academy offers year-round instruction to prepare the students for academic study in the U.S., with special attention to the reading, writing, listening and speaking skills that are needed to succeed. The faculty are ready to help the students learn the English skills necessary to succeed in a dynamic learning environment, and which will inspire, motivate, and prepare them to become leaders in today's global enterprise. "Successful completion of USC Language Academy courses does not guarantee admission to any degree program at the University of Southern California. All students must apply to university degree programs through the regular channels, including the

USC Office of Admission and individual departments" (University of Southern California, Language Academy 2010).At the Language Academy, small classes and individualized sessions provide customized services which help the international students grow comfortable in a new environment. Language learning happens both inside and outside the classroom, so the programs are designed to encourage learning in many settings and help the students take full advantage of their time at USC.

The Intensive English Program is tailored to the international students needs, from reading and writing to oral skills, grammar, and research assistance. These skills are embedded in the curriculum and enriched by language labs such as conversation partners, GRE/GMAT preparation, USC admissions advising, writing and grammar tutorials. The results are well-rounded students who are ready to face higher education, careers and global challenges.

Librarians collaborate with the Language Academy to design and conduct information literacy workshops for ESL students in the Academy's Intensive English Program. These two-hour information literary instruction sessions are offered once a semester and take place in hands-on networked computer classrooms. The class research assignment requires students to write a research paper and then make an oral presentation of pros and cons on their assigned topics. The overall theme is often a debate on a social issue, such as euthanasia, legalization of marijuana, or bilingual education. In the first hour of the two-hour session, the librarians teach the information research process, e.g. how to search and refine a topic, find and evaluate the scholarly sources, and retrieve the full-text. During the second hour of the session, the librarians work with students one-on-one to find sources for their specific research topics. Furthermore, the library's computer consultant conducts PowerPoint software training workshops to help students prepare their oral presentation.

East Asian Library (EAL)

East Asian librarians, upon request, provide tours, class presentations, and orientations to groups and students from Japanese, Korean and

Chinese-speaking countries. In addition, the librarians at the Korean Heritage Library take a rather unusual approach to reach out to East Asian students, particularly Korean students.

Housed in the East Asian Library, the Korean Heritage Library's materials constitute over 40% of the East Asian Library's collection. It is one of the leading Korean collections in North America, especially with respect to the Audio/Video collection, which is famous internationally. Users of the Korean Heritage are students and scholars from the USC Korean Studies Institute, USC Korean Studies scholars, Korean-American community, and Korean scholars from around the world. The majority of the students are graduate students majoring in Social Sciences and Humanities subject areas, especially, Social Work, Public Policy and Planning, Cinematic Arts, History, Political Science, Gerontology, Linguistics, and Literature.

Because of the large Korean user community they serve, the Korean librarians have utilized an innovative pedagogical strategy to respond to the information literacy needs of their students. Their sessions are called "Lunch and Learn at the Library" and take place over lunch in their native Korean language. The Library provides ethnic food and creates an environment that is close to students' home cultural background. These workshops focus on introducing students to resources and services at USC Libraries. The "Lunch and Learn at the Library" program began in 2004, and became popular in the first few years. Normally the Korean librarians offer two introductory sessions in the fall: one for graduate students and another for postdoctoral researchers and visiting scholars. The sessions are repeated in spring if there is a need. The fall introductory sessions are usually attended by 10–20 graduate students and 10 postdoctoral researchers and visiting scholars. The spring semester sessions are usually smaller, with about 10 attendees.

The program has been very successful and has had a positive impact on student learning. To assess the effectiveness of the sessions, the librarians use both formal and informal assessment mechanisms. At the end of "Lunch and Learn at the Library" sessions, the participants fill out an evaluation form. The evaluation form includes five questions on the following topics: 1) presentation format, 2) presentation content/information presented, 3) what they learned, 4) what they hoped to learn that was not covered, and 5) any suggestions for improvement. Comments reveal the popularity and effectiveness of the sessions and their importance to students' information literacy needs. Some students requested that these sessions become regular events at the beginning of semester every year for new graduate students. Students also suggested that the sessions provide time for hands-on practice by offering the instruction sessions in a computer lab classroom.

Informally, the effectiveness of the sessions are assessed in various ways, for example: students' oral comments, increased reference and consultation requests, increased circulation of books and DVDs (not only for themselves but for their family members), good rapport between students and librarians, and librarians being invited to students' events.

Furthermore, the Korean librarians collaborate with the USC's Korean Association for Social Sciences (KASS) student organization. The Association's mission is to promote social, intellectual, and cultural activities for Korean students and scholars in the fields of Social Sciences at USC. The membership includes Master or Doctoral program graduate students who are enrolled in the Social Sciences fields, as well as Postdoctoral fellows and visiting scholars who are doing research in these disciplines or related subject areas. Through outreach to KASS, the Curator of the Korean Heritage Library offers library instruction sessions to students in the Association with a concept of "food for mind and body." The Curator introduces students to the Library's services and Korean resources at USC and serves food and refreshments in the EAL Seminar room. The East Asian librarians hope to extend the Lunch and Learn instructional programs to all East Asian students, including Chinese and Japanese students.

Other Library Initiatives (Law and Dental)

For students in schools that offer their own departmental orientation programs, subject librarians make presentations at department and school orientation programs. For example, international students who have declared Dentistry, Medicine, or the allied health professions are required to participate in a variety of language development sessions at the American Language Institute prior to matriculation. The Wilson Dental Library, in coordination with the faculty and curriculum advisors, conducts orientation sessions for international students during their first trimester. These sessions start with a lecture, but end with hands-on exercises in order to support language learning and comprehension as well as computer skills. Throughout the first year, further hands-on sessions may be scheduled as needed. About 80 international dental students are enrolled each year.

The USC Gould School of Law offers a graduate Master's of Law (L.L.M.). This program is designed for international attorneys, judges, government officials, prosecutors, corporate legal counsels, bankers, and recent law graduates who are interested in studying the U.S. legal system and receiving a degree in American law. This new program enrolled 86 international students when it first started in 2008. The enrollment has continued to grow, and as of 2010 it has reached 131. The law librarians offer specially designed research workshops in hands-on computer classrooms for these international students.

Information Literacy and Technology

To complement in-classroom information literacy instruction, librarians adopt a wide range of new technologies, including LibGuides, self-paced tutorials and virtual reference services. Online tutorials provide opportunities for international students to learn on their own time and at their own pace about library concepts. It also allows them to review and refresh their skills as needed (Peters 2010).

The USC Libraries have adopted LibGuides to create subject research guides for users. For international students enrolled in different courses of the American Language Institute, the ALI research guide provides a one-stop virtual research portal (See Figure 13.2, http://libguides.usc.edu/ALI).

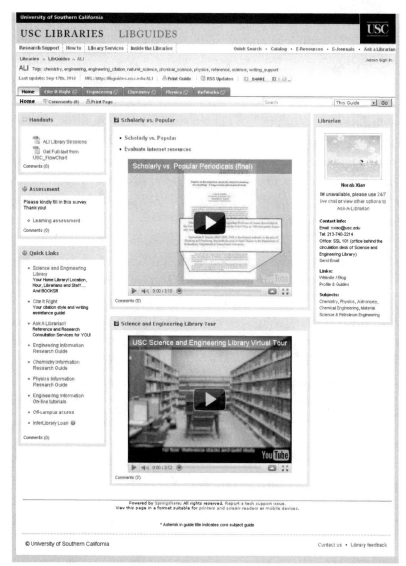

Figure 13.2: ALI LibGuide

Within this guide, students can find quick links to library resources and services, as well as virtually chat with a librarian. To optimize student learning from the two-hour session of information literacy instruction, many traditional components of the lesson plan are
transferred to this guide. For instance, students can view the virtual

tour of the Science and Engineering Library prepared in Camtasia on YouTube to familiarize themselves with the Library's physical layout, as well as get connected with people who will provide help. Additionally, students can retrieve electronic copies of class handouts from the research guide, including the "ALI library sessions" main handouts, and "Get Full-text from USC Flowchart." Since most of the students are from science or engineering disciplines, shortcut links to subject research guides are given as sub-pages. To help international students understand citations, improve their technical writing skills, and master citation management software, the guide links to two citation self-help guides, "Citation" and "RefWorks."

Furthermore, librarians have developed online tutorials for students (http://www.usc.edu/libraries/about/reference/tutorials/). Two self-paced tutorials, Research 101 and Academic Integrity, are especially important to international students. The first tutorial, *Research 101* (http://www.usc.edu/libraries/research101/), is an interactive tutorial that consists of six independent modules, each with its own set of objectives, information, and exercises. It is based upon content and design elements developed for Research 101 by University of Washington Libraries. The USC Libraries have modified this tutorial to offer a library-branded information literacy resource tailored to the USC Libraries learning environment.

The modules cover the basics of library research, such as how to develop a topic and research questions, select a source, conduct search, interpret citations, retrieve materials, and evaluate the source. The tutorial is not intended to replace the in-person class instructions, instead it complements bibliographic instruction and provides an alternative for students who wish to review and learn about the research process. It is now part of the ALI's academic curriculum. Students are required to take the tutorial prior to attending the library instruction session. Thus librarians can briefly review the basics and then focus on presenting advanced topics. *Research 101* was initially developed and piloted in spring 2007.

The second tutorial is *Academic Integrity*, an online self-paced tutorial prepared using Adobe Presenter and streamed from an Adobe

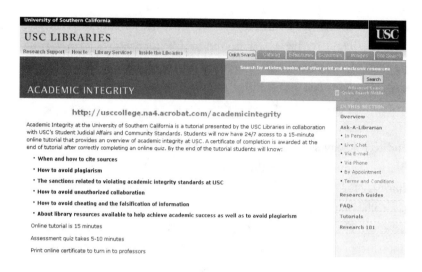

Figure 13.3: Academic Integrity

Connector server (See Figure 13.3, http://www.usc.edu/libraries/about/reference/tutorials/academic_integrity/index.php).

Plagiarism is often an issue for international students, in particular students from Asian and Middle Eastern cultures. In these societies, plagiarism is not viewed as illegal conduct like it is in Western cultures (Peters 2010). Glenn D. Deckert's (1993) study of Chinese students in a Hong Kong college revealed that these "students had little familiarity with the Western notion of plagiarism and poor ability to recognize it" (131), and concluded that "students need explicit orientation and training on how to avoid plagiarism when writing in a Western academic community" (131). Baron and Strout-Dapaz's (2001) information literacy standards for international students further emphasize the ACRL Information Literacy Competency Standard of understanding "many of the economic, legal and social issues surrounding the use of information and access" and using "information ethically and legally" (319).

In this 15-minute tutorial, students become aware of academic integrity as defined by USC's Student Judicial Affairs and Community Standards. After taking the tutorial, students are required to complete an online quiz, which takes about 5–10 minutes, and if they answer all questions correctly, a certificate of completion is awarded. International students, who have little background in this important academic issue, particularly welcome this tutorial. With these two tutorials, international students are prepared for the next stage of information literacy instruction at USC.

International students also have opportunities to hone their research and technology skills by accessing on-line reference tutorials at the Library's Tutorials website (http://www.usc.edu/libraries/about/reference/tutorials/). These tutorials are created using Camtasia software, through the collaborative efforts of librarians and are well received by users. Students can also find links to commercial tutorials from publishers and vendors (http://www.usc.edu/libraries/about/reference/tutorials/equipment/).

In addition to the above-mentioned customized research guides and self-paced tutorials, the Libraries have provided many more innovative library services to the USC community. Students can get reference and research help by email, phone, in-person, and via chat. In fact, USC users are served with three kinds of chat: OCLC QuestionPoint Cooperative Chat, USC Local IM Chat service via Pidgin (http://www.libraryh3lp.com), and several Subject-Based Local Chat systems on LibGuides. These diverse chat services provide reference and research assistance at the point and time of need.

Conclusion

The USC Libraries long-standing history of collaboration with university-wide programs has helped broaden our outreach to international students. Through our collaboration with the Office of Orientation Programs, the American Language Institute, and the Language Academy, library programs are systematically integrated into international students' academic curricula. The USC Libraries benefit from the public relations and communications that go to all international students registered at USC.

In the future, we look forward to expanding collaboration and enhancing integration. The Academic Integrity Tutorial is being redesigned and will be included in the mandatory online activities, which all students, including international students, must complete before attending on-campus orientation programs. We expect to expand our information literacy programs with different academic departments and to various language and culture groups. The model used by the librarians at the Korean Heritage Library could also be adapted to reach Japanese- and Chinese-speaking students. We will continue to build on these and other opportunities that arise to become systematically integrated into the research programs, teaching curricula, and learning activities of our users. As stated in the USC Libraries Strategic Plan "*The Essential Library 2011–2013*" (USC Libraries 2011),

"The USC Libraries will be an innovative, inspiring, and integral partner in the scholarly achievements of USC faculty, students, and staff. In so doing, we actively contribute to the development of knowledge and the advancement of society."

References

Baron, Sara and Alexia Strout-Dapaz. 2001. "Communicating with and Empowering International Students with a Library Skills Set." *Reference Services Review* 29 (4): 314–326.

Business Week. 2009. "Top Undergraduate Business Programs." http://www.businessweek.com/interactive_reports/undergrad_bschool_2009.html

Deckert, Glenn D. 1993. "Perspectives on Plagiarism from ESL Students in Hong Kong." *Journal of Second Language Writing* 2 (2): 131–148.

Peters, Anne E. 2010. *International Students and Academic Libraries: A Survey of Issues and Annotated Bibliography*. Lanham, Md.: Scarecrow Press.

University of Southern California Libraries. 2010. *Orientation Evaluation: Graduate and International Students, August 2010 (Internal Report)*.

University of Southern California, American Language Institute. 2010. *Credit Program Statistical Report, Academic Year 2009–2010 (Internal Report)*.

University of Southern California, Language Academy. 2010. *The USC Language Academy Intensive English Program*. http://www.usc.edu.libproxy.usc.edu/dept/education/langacad/downloads/LA_viewbook_HIres.pdf.

University of Southern California, Office of International Services. 2010. *International Student Enrollment Report, Fall 2009*. http://sait.usc.edu.libproxy.usc.edu/ois/Upload/Publications/EnrollmentReport/2009-2010%20ER.pdf.

USC Libraries. 2011. *The Essential Library 2011–2013*. http://www.usc.edu.libproxy.usc.edu/libraries/essential/

U.S. News and World Report. 2009. "America's Best Colleges." http://colleges.usnews.rankingsandreviews.com/best-colleges/

About the Editors

Pamela A. Jackson is the Information Literacy Librarian at San Diego State University (SDSU). She has been active in outreach to diverse student populations, planning library support for international students, and coordinating interactive online library education. In her career as an academic librarian, she has contributed to international student success through a variety of roles including service as the Global and International Library Programs Coordinator; Global Studies Faculty Advisory Committee Member; library coordinator for a proposed joint program with El Salvador; and by organizing instructional visits, library tours, specialized handouts, an online tutorial, and a hands-on library activity for international students studying in the United States. She has published survey research about incoming international students and their library needs, and has conducted comparative research assessing domestic and international students' understanding of plagiarism. Ms. Jackson is a member of Phi Beta Delta Honor Society for International Scholars. She holds a M.A. in Library and Information Studies from the University of Wisconsin-Madison and a M.A. in English from Sonoma State University.

Patrick Sullivan has worked extensively with international students since entering the library field. He is actively involved in the local San Diego State University (SDSU) Scholars Without Borders and previously with Phi Beta Delta International Scholars Society. His work has included focused instructional activities primarily with international business students here in the United States, but he has also acted as the library liaison to international students at San Diego State University. Mr. Sullivan received a Fulbright Garcia-Robles Scholarship to better connect libraries and librarians in the Baja California region and to work as a founding member of the Baja California Library Association.

He continues to work extensively with the national Mexican Library Association as a member of their International Relations Committee. He is the current chair of ALA's Americas Subcommittee within the International Relations Committee. He has presented internationally on topics such as virtual reference, sister libraries, and search and retrieval techniques. He is currently the Business Reference Librarian at San Diego State University.